THE PEOPLE PRINCIPLES

Leadership in the 21st Century

Mark J. Balzer

AuthorHouse™
1663 Liberty Drive
Bloomington, IN 47403
www.authorhouse.com
Phone: 1-800-839-8640

© 2011 Mark J. Balzer. All rights reserved.

No part of this book may be reproduced, stored in a retrieval system, or transmitted by any means without the written permission of the author.

First published by AuthorHouse 5/31/2011

ISBN: 978-1-4567-5908-7 (sc)
ISBN: 978-1-4567-5909-4 (hc)
ISBN: 978-1-4567-5910-0 (e)

Printed in the United States of America

Any people depicted in stock imagery provided by Thinkstock are models, and such images are being used for illustrative purposes only. Certain stock imagery © Thinkstock.

This book is printed on acid-free paper.

Because of the dynamic nature of the Internet, any web addresses or links contained in this book may have changed since publication and may no longer be valid. The views expressed in this work are solely those of the author and do not necessarily reflect the views of the publisher, and the publisher hereby disclaims any responsibility for them.

Contents

Foreword		vii
Introduction		ix
Chapter One	The Dilemma	1
Chapter Two	The Challenge	8
Chapter Three	The Plan	12
Chapter Four	M&Ms	23
Chapter Five	The Wizard of Oz	56
Chapter Six	Fishing Lures	80
Chapter Seven	Rosetta Stone	98
Chapter Eight	Green Beans	121
Chapter Nine	Milk Bones	136
Chapter Ten	Twenty Dollar Bill	156
Chapter Eleven	(S+A = B) = O	183
Conclusion	Pay it forward	195
Afterward		204
Acknowledgements		205

FOREWORD

It has been a privilege to have had the opportunity to work with Mark Balzer over the last 15 years. This book is a culmination of experience and insight that have resulted in a very successful career, both for Mark and for those under his tutelage during this time. Through the time that I have been exposed to his work, he has truly developed sensitivity to the integrity of the individual and the essential qualities required to lead in today's diverse and challenging work environments.

Mark comes to the table as a leader who has taken the time to learn operations, and has tailored the Human Resource and Training Departments under his authority to meet the real needs of work environments today. Over the last several years, I have watched Mark build one of the most successfully integrated development training programs I have been exposed to, and have personally learned lessons in my own development in operational leadership through my association with him.

In writing this book, he has creatively crafted a story line that brings the essentials of successful leadership to the forefront, teaching these principles in a very understandable and entertaining fashion. The book outlines the proper sequence of steps necessary to establish the required fundamental foundation of being an effective leader.

The reader will find that the format lends itself equally well to the development of an individual or a team. The principles in this book are applicable to all levels within an organization – from a senior executive level to front-line supervision. It will provide interactive discussion points for operational staff meetings as well as a formal training platform.

Application of the tools in this guide will build a productive and, most importantly, an engaged workforce and leadership team. Even a currently highly efficient and effective team will experience positive incremental growth as a result. The principles will also undergird the essential, though often elusive, result of ongoing improvement.

Enjoy the read, and most importantly, use the materials to reflect on your own style and practices. Both you and your organization will benefit from what can be learned here.

                                          Phillip Kohn
                                          General Manager
                                          Exel, Inc

Introduction

Leadership is not for the faint at heart. It takes courage to lead others. Of all the endeavors I have ever attempted to master in my life, being a leader is by far the most challenging. It is not a process you can work on every once in a while; on the contrary, it requires a daily commitment to your team, the organization that employs you, and yourself. It requires discipline to change one's behavior, attitude, and philosophy surrounding one's role in the organization. Leaders and managers are quite different. This is not to suggest that leaders do not need to know how to plan, organize, direct, and control, but people expect more from the people they report to than the four primary roles of management. Leadership is beyond management. It is the positive and willing influence of others.

Over the past twenty-five years, I have trained thousands of people on the discipline of leadership and the impact leaders can have on the people they lead. It thrills me to think of the number of people that have transformed themselves from manager to leader, and their impact on other individuals as well as the organization as a result of the training: not only in terms of the growth of those individuals, but also the growth of the people they lead. It is amazing how leadership energizes an entire team.

But it also saddens me to think of the number of people who lack the discipline to make the changes necessary to become a leader, not only because of how they suffer, but because of the negative impact it has on their team. I truly feel sad for the people that work for these individuals. People deserve more than management. They deserve leadership.

I have been asked by many people in my training classes over the years to write a book; two years ago I began to put my thoughts on leadership down on paper. *The People Principles* is a leadership fable that has allowed me to convey my beliefs and philosophy on leaders and their behavior. The characters and events in the fable are an amalgamation of the real and events and experiences I have encountered in my career in Human Resources and Training and Development.

I hope you will enjoy reading the book as much as I enjoyed writing it. So sit back, grab a pen or pencil to take notes, and enjoy the fascinating study of leadership.

Chapter One
The Dilemma

Steve Gugino, the General Manager of Dunkirk Distribution Company, was nervously pacing in his office. He was waiting for Bill Crocoll to arrive for a meeting to discuss the development plan for a new college hire at the facility. Bill, the facility's HR manager had been out of the office for two months working on a troubled start-up in Ontario, California. Steve fidgeted with a stack of papers on his desk, feeling his anxiety increase with each passing minute. Steve was not known in the company for his patience.

Staring out of his window to the parking lot of the building, Steve replayed a recent conversation with his manager in his mind. The development of Randy Sysol was critical to both of their careers. Steve couldn't help but think of all he had contributed to the business throughout his career -- and now his career was being jeopardized by a twenty-two-year-old college hire. He was having a difficult time justifying that to himself. Were all his past accomplishments for nothing? Why didn't they factor into the equation? He knew college recruiting was important to the business, but this situation took the significance of the program to a whole new level. He could not believe how important the development of Randy was to company, let alone him. *Randy's just one of fifty students the company's recruited recently,* Steve kept thinking. *Misplaced priorities.*

His manager had explained in no uncertain terms that Randy had to be successful in his role, and Steve was going to be held accountable for ensuring that outcome. The phrase "Failure is not an option" echoed in his head. He couldn't help but feel sorry for himself. With all the demands of the business, and seasonal volume spike about to hit, the last thing he needed was the pressure and accountability of developing some hot shot college graduate.

Mark J. Balzer

Randy was a recent college hire assigned to Steve's building, who had been personally interviewed by Sean Murphy, the president of the company. Randy, a 3.9 GPA student from Iowa State University with a Bachelor's degree in distribution and logistics, was considered the cream of the crop among the company's recent spring college recruits. The president considered him a "can't miss" candidate, the type of person the company needed to grow the business and increase its competitive edge in the marketplace. It was rumored that Murphy saw a lot of himself in Randy: a smart, aggressive, small town boy looking to do well in the big city. *Give me a break; if Randy's so important to the business, he should report directly to Murphy,* Steve thought to himself.

Dunkirk Distribution was part of Globalistics, a world leader in third party distribution. Recruiting top college talent was part of the company's long-term strategic goals in supporting the anticipated growth of the business. Murphy felt college recruiting was the lifeblood of the organization and would ensure a competitive advantage over other third-party distribution companies in the future. The president had expressed concerns about the increased turnover of recent college hires, and placed the blame for it on leaders not making the development of new college hires a high enough priority. Murphy had gotten engaged at all levels of the college recruiting program, making it a top business initiative for all executives at Globalistics. He was known in the company as a brilliant strategist who rose quickly through the ranks, and he was well-respected at all levels of the organization. He was also known for his tenacity in meeting financial results for the shareholders; when he put his attention to an issue, it was a given that success would follow. Everyone in the company knew Murphy did not like to be disappointed. The man hated losing more than he enjoyed winning. Murphy was determined that college recruiting would be successful -- *or else.*

The company's goal was to recruit one hundred college students per year into entry- level leadership positions. Meeting this target was part of every executive's bonus plan, and this trickled down to the performance objectives for directors and general managers as well. The company had invested hundreds of thousands of dollars into the program; both the placement and the development of each college hire had high visibility for the senior leadership team. If a college student was placed in your facility, as the general manager of the site, you were accountable for their success. Randy's placement had even higher visibility than most because Murphy had personally handpicked Dunkirk Distribution as the location for Randy's entry into the organization. Murphy had started his career with Globalistics at Dunkirk himself, though Dunkirk Distribution had changed dramatically since Murphy worked there. The size of the building had increased from 150,000 thousand square feet to 1.2 million square feet, and the volume had increased by five times.

Why me? Steve thought.

He turned away from the window, returned to his desk, and pulled out his notes regarding Randy Sysol and his past two months at Dunkirk. Steve remembered sensing a bit of arrogance in Randy during their initial interactions, but chalked it up to Randy trying to impress his new boss. He knew Randy was very intelligent, but wondered if he would be able to relate to his employees. Steve knew that leadership started and ended with people, and he wasn't sure Randy placed a premium on people. He was a nice young man, and Steve coached him on the importance of employee relations, emphasizing that being successful in business was not just about having the technical skills to complete a task, but even more importantly, about being able to develop relationships with the people that worked for him. Steve had his doubts, though, about whether Randy had really grasped that concept. *Is the phrase "People matter" so hard to understand?* Steve wondered. Early reports of Randy's progress as a leader were not encouraging. He was seen as standoffish and as a bit of a task master by his team.

Randy had started at the facility two months ago, and these first months had been less than stellar. His behavior towards the hourly associates on his team had caused major disruptions in the building -- and his team was comprised of some of the most senior and valuable people on the floor. Most of Randy's team had more than fifteen years of experience with the company and had made significant contributions to the success of the facility over the years. Steve had personally supervised many of the people on Randy's team when he started at the facility as an operations manager eight years earlier. He found them to be hard-working people, and reasonable on most issues. Steve had specifically assigned Randy to lead this team because he knew them: this team could make any leader successful. Steve had thought that assigning him that team was a fail-proof solution: all he had to do was open the doors and stay out of their way. Steve was surprised and disappointed when he learned that these people were unhappy within the first month of having Randy as a supervisor. You really had to work hard to make these people unhappy. He thought, *I should have let Randy's manager write him up and get him out of the building,* but he knew that would have been political suicide. Yet he also knew that he would have fired any other leader who behaved like Randy.

Steve looked at his watch, still thinking hard. The complaints from Randy's team ranged from his arrogance and disrespect towards them to his total disregard for their experience and knowledge, which had helped to make the facility the top producer in the company's supply chain network of more than three hundred locations. Randy's mantra of "that's old-school thinking" irritated the entire team, enough that many of them had expressed their frustration and anger to Steve. These associates were people whom Steve valued and respected, and weren't known as complainers. They had worked under many different supervisors over the years and had actually helped other supervisors to understand the business and advance their careers. This team made every other supervisor look like a top performer in the building – except for Murphy's hot-shot from Iowa State. These types of issues were unusual at Dunkirk Distribution. Most of the time, the leadership and hourly employees worked together very well and without the all-too-common "us versus them" mentality that many businesses had to deal with.

Steve knew Randy was digging a hole and that if it got much bigger, he would not be able to get out. Randy's acclimation to the company was not going well, and immediate action was required. He knew the time commitment required to turn Randy around was great, and the coming seasonal volume spike would not allow him sufficient time to coach Randy.

Steve also knew the person that could help Randy the most was Bill, who was returning today from the Dutton Enterprise start-up. As far as Steve was concerned, Bill couldn't get to his office soon enough. The issue needed to be addressed immediately. Steve glanced at his watch again and muttered out loud, "Bill, where are you?"

Steve was not a big fan of HR in general. He felt most HR professionals were prima donnas: a bunch of administrators with little knowledge of the business, they simply hid behind the policy manual. People that can, do, and people that can't, work in HR. Maybe it was an unfair appraisal of the HR profession, but Steve viewed HR as overhead cost, adding nothing to the bottom line, and creators of a never ending flow of meaningless forms with no real impact on the business.

But he did not view Bill in this way. Bill was his type of HR person. He was all about making the business better, not about pushing an HR agenda. Bill could explain Labor Management Standards as well as he could explain the Family Medical Leave Act. He spoke the language of operations and knew the business as well as most operations people. He wasn't a "desk jockey" like other HR people; he spent the majority of his time on the floor. He understood the business, the numbers, KPI's, challenges; heck, he was even forklift certified. Bill was an extraordinary human resources professional in Steve's eyes and was known throughout the business as the ultimate "people person."

Bill had started at Globalistics right out of college as a floor operations supervisor, but his ability to relate with people at all levels of the organization caught the eye of Jerry Phelps, the Senior Vice President of human resources at the time. After Bill had spent five years as a supervisor, Jerry finally persuaded him to join the human resources team. Bill never bought into the HR-by-the-book mentality; he was a business leader working in the HR field. His philosophy was simple: know the business, speak operation's language, not "HR talk," partner with your customers, and contribute to the bottom line. He wasn't happy with a seat at the table; he wanted a voice at the table, and he earned one. He believed in eliminating unnecessary HR for HR sake and he knew the secret language operators understood: drive efficiencies into the business and waste out of it. If HR could eliminate work from an operator's plate or remove costs from the operations, operators would listen. He wasn't always well-received by his peers in HR, but the folks in operations genuinely liked and respected him.

Steve took a sip of his coffee and swiveled his chair to look out the window. His thoughts drifted back and forth between his current dilemma and his impatience for Bill's arrival. He thought about calling him, but did not want to come across as desperate. Gazing intently out of the window as if he might find some answers out there, he started thinking again about Bill's strengths. In addition to his knowledge of the business, Bill had the ability to make every person he came into contact with feel important, and always left them smiling. He never forgot his roots. He was raised in a lower middle class family, and all the success he enjoyed during his career never changed his core values. The hourly employees at Dunkirk Distribution loved him. They knew Bill would always listen to their concerns. He wouldn't always agree with them, but people always felt they had received a fair shake. He knew every employee by name, and something personal about each of them. Steve couldn't remember ever hearing any negative feedback on Bill.

Bill had a Master's degree in organizational behavior from Mercyhurst University, but people often remarked that he also had a PhD in people from the school of life. He was a great coach and developer of people. Many leaders at Globalistics could attribute a part of their success to Bill's mentoring and training. Bill had passed on many opportunities to move up in the company; he was extremely family-oriented and was not willing to relocate his family to Frederick, Maryland, where the corporate office was located. He enjoyed the small town feeling of Dunkirk. Besides, Bill wasn't in to titles. "People follow people, not titles" was his motto. His worth as a person was not determined by his level in the organization, but by the hearts he touched.

A loud knock on his door made him jump, almost spilling his coffee, and a voice bellowed, "What is so important that a man can't even have a cup of coffee without his boss starting to leave him frantic voicemails? I leave this place for a few months, and the whole thing falls apart."

Steve whirled his chair around to see Bill Crocoll grinning in his office doorway. Half smiling, but still with a sense of urgency, Steve replied, "You scared me to death. Hope you finished your work in Ontario, because you are definitely not going back out there. I need you here. I never should have volunteered you to help out with that start-up. Grab a cup of coffee if you like and then please have a seat with me over here." He pointed toward the round table at the back of his office.

Chapter Two
The Challenge

Bill had worked with Steve for eight years, and he had rarely seen Steve so tense. Steve was usually very laid-back and liked to spend a little quality personal time with people before getting to the business discussion. He was impatient but never rude, but his tone today was on the verge of rudeness. Bill knew by the look on Steve's face and tone of his voice that the issue was serious.

As Bill took a seat at the table, Steve wasted no time on small talk. "Sorry for the voicemail, but I really need your help with our new college hire. A young man named Randy Sysol. He hasn't gotten off to a great start." Steve continued to outline the entire situation in detail. Everything from Murphy's handpicking Randy for the site, to his referring to everyone and everything as "old school," to the complaints from the people on the floor. "So as you can see we have quite a challenge in front of us," Steve finished. Bill could gauge the severity of the issue in Steve's strained voice and the look on his face.

Bill took a sip of his coffee and then just held it in his hands, not responding right away. He quietly digested Steve's concerns for a moment, thinking through the situation. He could sense that Steve was becoming impatient for his response, but he wanted to provide the best possible counsel to Steve. He knew Steve was looking for a lifeline, and his response needed to give him hope.

He sat up in his chair, leaned forward to set his cup down and rested his elbows on the table, and then spoke in a very calm but direct voice. "Steve, I agree the situation needs to be addressed immediately, but we need to be careful as we design a development plan for Randy. If we move too fast, without a detailed idea of where we're going, we could actually make the situation worse. The most important aspect of the plan will be Randy's mentor, so the first thing we need to do is review the leadership team and pick the best person for Randy's personality and needs." Bill could see his words were hitting their mark as the muscles in Steve's face began to relax. The tension in the room seemed to dissipate slightly.

"I've already evaluated the team," Steve told him. "I think I've settled on the best person to mentor Randy." Bill nodded expectantly. "He's sitting right in front of me."

Bill sat speechless, considering Steve's proposal and feeling his heart beat faster. He hadn't been on the floor as an Ops guy for years, and besides he'd been gone for all these months and had some serious catching up to do. He knew he had to say something, because Steve was at his wits end. He needed to find the words to let Steve down gently. "Steve, I would be more than happy to assist in developing the plan, and even with the mentoring at some level, but I'm an HR Manager, not a distribution guru. I haven't been on the floor in years, and we have other people on the team better qualified to help Randy than me. I think Randy would be best served by having an operations mentor. I haven't even met the young man yet, and I'm sure he has bonded with someone else already." Steve started to answer, but Bill continued firmly, "If he's as sharp as you say he is, and that headstrong, I'm not sure he would respect my counsel anyway. Do you think Randy would really listen to an HR guy? I sure wouldn't warm up to one of your operations guys coaching me on the finer points of human resources. But I'd be happy to work with whomever you pick as his mentor, and help however I can from the sidelines."

Steve took a sip of coffee, smiling, and let Bill finished his argument. Then he responded, "First of all, you aren't one of those HR guys. You started on the floor, and you understand the business better than most of the operations guys here, so that argument doesn't fly, my friend. I understand and appreciate your concerns, but Randy is not failing because of his lack of operational knowledge. He's failing because he has no people skills. If I've told him once, I've told him twenty times: the people in this building matter. He doesn't understand the leadership equation!" Steve paused momentarily to take a deep breath and regain his composure. "Eighty percent of leadership involves people. His world is productivity, productivity, productivity; nothing else. He needs a heavy dose of people leadership, and I cannot think of a better people person in this facility than you. You have a special way with people, and our leadership team performs so well today in a large part thanks to your influence. I've made the decision already. You're the guy."

Steve picked up his notes on Randy and handed them to Bill. "Just teach him everything you know about people." Bill began glancing through them as Steve added nonchalantly, "Besides, you were telling me before you went to California that you need a new challenge. Well, here you go. What I need you to do is develop a plan by 5:00 p.m. today, so that we can review it prior to your first meeting with Randy."

Bill looked up from his notes, and raising his voice slightly, asked, "What meeting with Randy? And 5:00 p.m. is not realistic."

Steve stood up and grabbed his day timer from his desk, disregarding Bill's concern, and explained, "I took the liberty of scheduling a meeting with Randy for tomorrow at 9:00 a.m. I realize you would like more time to prepare, but Randy is digging a hole so deep, it has to be handled immediately. I do feel bad about needing the plan by 5:00 today, but I need to give Karnes an update at six. I have a boss too, my friend. Besides, his credibility won't survive another week, and with the seasonal spike coming, we need our people focused on their jobs, not on Randy. So as you can see, we have a lot of work to get done. Bill, you're not writing this down. Are we on the same page?"

Bill took a deep breath. He had worked with Steve long enough to know that once he made a decision, he didn't change his mind, and he was on the hook for Randy's development. Trying to ask for more time or to get off the project would be futile. "Okay. Let me write down those times and what you need. Also, will you send me a copy of your notes about Randy's last two months here?" Standing up, he added wryly, "I appreciate the fact that you listened to my needs about wanting a new challenge, and giving me this wonderful opportunity. I'm not sure I can ever repay you for this one, boss. It always amazes me, what you hear and don't hear!"

The two men shook hands and as Bill walked out of the office, shaking his head the whole way, Steve called out, "Oh, yeah. And welcome back to Dunkirk!"

Chapter Three
The Plan

When Bill returned to his office and grabbed the cup of coffee he hadn't had time for because of Steve's frantic voicemail, he found the red light on his phone blinking, indicating that his mailbox was full. *Great,* he thought. *First day back in the office in two months, over twenty phone calls, who knows how many emails, the hiring plan for the quarter-end push to review, and now a new project with visibility all the way up to the president.* Bill was beginning to feel overwhelmed by the amount of work on his plate. *Don't just sit there,* he told to himself. *Do something.*

As he began reading his emails, he found himself muttering repeatedly, "Teach him everything I know about people." He wasn't even sure what that meant. This should get a great laugh at the Falcon Club on card night. *"What are you working on, Bill?" "Teaching someone everything I know about people." I know the punch line now: "Okay, but what do you do for the other seven hours and fifty five minutes at work?"* He was really struggling to frame up what needed to be done. He'd never really thought about what he knew about people, and now he had to teach a college-age hot-shot how to be a people person. *I should have stayed in Ontario.*

After he'd replied to all of his emails and finished returning his last phone call, Bill checked his watch and was surprised to discover it was already eleven o'clock. A faint sense of despair settled over him as he wondered where his morning had gone. His concentration was broken by a knock on the door. Standing at the door was Tammy Larkins, the human resources supervisor for the building.

Holding a notebook and some papers, Tammy walked into the office and sat down. "Well, boss, welcome back from Ontario. We sure missed you around here. I have a list of questions and issues that we need to cover. I was hoping we could use some of our one-on-one time to go over them?" She could tell by the look on his face that he was surprised to see her, she suspected he had had forgotten their monthly meeting. "Bill, it is the third Monday of the month, right? Did you forget, or do I have the wrong date?"

Bill looked at his desk calendar and then looked back at Tammy. "No," he assured her, "this is the third Monday of the month, and eleven a.m. is our meeting time. I'm just swamped today, and I completely forgot about the meeting. Tammy, I hope you don't mind, but I need to cancel today. Perhaps you can get with Margie to talk over your questions and issues, because I just don't have the time this week."

Tammy's smile turned into an expression of concern. "No, it's okay. I understand. I'll give Margie a call to see if she can help, and if there's something she can't answer, I'll email you. Just shoot me a meeting notice to reschedule our one-on-one."

Bill felt terrible about canceling the meeting. "Thanks for understanding," he said apologetically. "I'll make sure I respond to your emails. And I'll get back to you on the meeting, but it may be a while, because I have a huge project to complete."

Bill stood and walked Tammy to the door; as they shook hands, Bill could see the disappointment in her eyes, *What can I do?* he thought. *I really do want to talk with Tammy, but I have a limited amount of time, and this project has to take precedence over her. I'll make it up to her later.*

Not feeling great about canceling the meeting with Tammy, Bill returned to his desk, took out a pad of paper, and titled the first page, "What I know about people." He took a sip of his coffee, enjoying the feeling of the warm cup in his hand; still holding the cup, he leaned back in his chair and began to think about the question. He loved working with people, even though at times it involved some conflict and petty drama; working with people was rewarding and always gave him new insights. One thing he had learned was that people need to know they matter: they need to know they're more than just an object of labor. Bill leaned forward, set his cup down, and picked up his pen. He began writing on his tablet: "People are our most important asset." As he read what he had written, he thought about his conversation with Tammy, and before he knew it, he was dialing her extension. His conscience had gotten the best of him. *How can I stress that people are our most important resource to Randy, yet not employ this concept myself?* He knew the answer to his question. *Crocoll, you need to practice what you preach.*

He heard Tammy's voice over the speakerphone and immediately picked up the handset. "Tammy, are you still in the building? Good! I rearranged my schedule and I can still make our meeting if you are available. Can you meet me in the parking lot? Let's have lunch at the Covered Wagon, and you can catch me up on the business." As he hung up the phone, the smile returned to his face and he underlined the sentence on the sheet of paper: "People are our most important asset." He thought to himself, *This is one thing I know for sure about people.* He put down his pen and headed toward the elevator, one step closer to a plan for Randy.

As he and Tammy drove down Central Avenue in his Honda Accord, Bill explained his meeting with Steve and what he had been asked to do. He found himself relaxing; talking to Tammy seemed to relieve some of the pressure. As Bill finished, Tammy told him, "This is really a coincidence – Randy's behavior was one of the things that I wanted to talk to you about." Steve gave Tammy a small smile as she continued with her thoughts. "Steve is right: Randy has caused quite a stir on the floor. People are getting tired of his abruptness with them. No, I think it's past being abrupt – it's rude! You know our folks," she added kindly. "Overall we have a great bunch of people: very diverse, and hard-working, and just generally very respectful. However, Randy has managed in just two short months to cause a major uproar. Even Pam and Molly are upset, and it takes something major for them to complain. Think about that, Bill – Pam and Molly, two of the most calm, good-natured people in the facility, are angry. That sure raised a red flag in my mind. I can't believe Steve stopped

Randy's write-up. Steve keeps telling us to try to work with him – work with him, give me a break! I think we should cut our losses and fire him."

Bill was beginning to grasp the gravity of the situation. He knew there was a problem, but initially had felt that Steve's emotions might have had an impact his objectivity in communicating the severity of the matter. Listening to Tammy, whom he knew to be extremely level-headed and a clear thinker, he realized that Randy's problem was much larger than he had first anticipated. If Tammy wanted Steve to fire him, it must be bad. Steve may have even understated the issue.

He shook his head in disbelief. "Wow – if Pam and Molly are upset, things must be really bad. Those two are the most laid-back, even-keeled people I know. Honestly, I can't remember them ever getting upset about anything. This isn't a red flag; this is an earthquake." Bill turned the car into the parking lot at the Covered Wagon. "Tammy, how is this possible? How can one person cause so much damage in two months? What exactly has Randy done?"

As they walked to the entrance of the restaurant Tammy explained in tones of exasperation, "It's his total lack of appreciation for their work and life experience. They've been in the inventory department for over ten years, and just the other day, Randy changed the cycle counting process without talking to them first. They tried to explain the current process and why it was implemented in the first place, and how the change could affect the pick accuracy of the lines. Without listening to a word they said, he told them their thinking was old school, and that there are new ways of doing things in the new millennium. They pushed back, but Randy just told them point blank, he was in charge and if they wanted to keep their jobs, they would implement his changes. He threatened to fire two of our best people; the nerve of this kid! Can you believe how he talked to them?" Tammy shook her head in frustration.

Bill said, concerned, "Steve mentioned his catchphrase of 'old school' during our meeting this morning when we discussed Randy's shortcomings. Sounds like he missed the lecture on people leadership in college; the technical component of the job is the easy part, but the people side of the leadership equation is where you get real results." Bill opened the door to the restaurant to let Tammy go in first. The hostess asked if it was just the two of them, and led them to a table. It was clear that they were both in deep thought as they looked over the menu.

When the waitress came to take their drink order, Tammy said, "I'm ready to order if you are, Bill; I know you need to get back to the office."

Bill laid down his menu. "I'm good." He let Tammy order first, and then he ordered himself. The waitress picked up both menus and left.

Now they were free to continue their conversation. Bill wanted to find something positive about Randy, some hint of leadership skills. "Tammy, he must have some positive characteristics," he suggested.

Wanting to be fair to Randy's situation, Tammy hesitated for a moment, spreading her napkin on her lap. "Let me think about that." She took a deep breath to regain her composure. "Randy has gotten under my skin, but to be fair, he is an incredibly bright individual, he's very ambitious, and he knows distribution inside and out. In one-on-one interactions, he comes across as very polite and respectful. I had a very positive first impression when I met him. I can see why we hired him. I really thought, what a great young leader." She paused again, collecting her thoughts as the waitress brought their drinks. "But once he gets on the floor, he's an entirely different person. Like a Doctor Jekyll and Mr. Hyde personality change. He has this dark side to him. He wants to be successful and has the drive to do so, but he doesn't know how to build relationships. He's a bull in a china shop: get out of his way, because this guy is driven to succeed. I'm not sure he understands the impact his behavior has on his team. He reminds me of Tim Bender. Remember him? Great technical ability, and horrible people skills?"

Bill gave a slight chuckle and sat back in his chair. "Tim Bender, now there's a blast from the past. Never met a person with more technical knowledge of a warehouse than him, but he broke glass with everyone he came in contact with. He could never just have a simple, everyday conversation with his team. If it wasn't business related he didn't want to hear about it. Never saw anything like it. I talked to him so many times about his people skills before we terminated him. He always told me, 'People should be here to work. Period.' He wasn't into the 'touchy-feely HR stuff,' and I could not get him to realize that a major portion of his job was human resources, and the development of his people. Tim only focused on trucks in and trucks out. It was a shame, because he had so much knowledge, he was just stuck in his ways. Now *he* was 'old school'," Bill laughed, taking a sip of his diet Coke. "Tammy, this young man cannot be as bad as Tim Bender."

Tammy set her glass down and replied, "Well, not yet. But he's going down the same path as Tim. Bill, my biggest concern with Randy is, I don't think he has any clue what he's done on the floor. I think he's under the impression he's doing a great job. I have discussed his performance with him twice and stressed our leadership philosophy with people. He just shakes his head yes then does the opposite. I have my doubts about whether he can be turned around. Do you think you can get him on the right track?"

Bill smiled and shook his head. "I do," he said, and then paused as the waitress brought their food, so that they could both say thank you as she walked away. He continued, "I do think we have a chance to turn Randy around. He's bright; we just need to get him to see how his behavior is impacting the team. Plus, you know my philosophy: never give up on people. In my career, people continue to amaze me when I least expect it. He has a lot of positive attributes; we just need to get him to see the big picture. It's all about the people, and too often, people are so concerned with the business that they fail to realize the importance of building relationships with others. Besides, he's at a different point in his career than Tim was. Hopefully his behavior is not already ingrained into his brain."

Tammy nodded. "That's a good point; he is at a different place in his career than Tim was. But my biggest concern is Randy's ego. You haven't met him yet. He's very self-assured, even arrogant at times. I hope he'll listen to you, and lets himself examine his behavior. He sure didn't listen to me."

Bill swallowed a bite of food and leaned back in his chair. He smiled and agreed, "Tammy, sometimes a person's ego is their own worst enemy. I've often seen talented people fail when ego gets in the way. We need to focus on his desire for success and show him how his behavior is undermining that goal. We need to reach his heart. Logic makes people think, but emotions make people act. We need to develop a plan to show him the negative impact his current behavior is having on the team, without destroying his sense of his worth. We have to somehow make it *his* plan, not our plan. I've seen young leaders dig themselves into such a big hole that they can't ever recover. What's the size of his?"

Tammy looked down at her plate. "He would have to get on his tippy toes to look over the edge."

Bill murmured, half to himself, "It's one of the saddest things to witness. When you start leading a team, you don't have much time to establish rapport and credibility with them. From day one, you're either climbing or digging – there's no such thing as status quo." He cleared his throat. "Thanks for your candor, Tammy; you've given me good insight on what I'm up against. Let's discuss my project for a minute. Steve wants me to teach Randy 'everything I know about people,' and I'm not even sure what that means." Bill looked thoughtfully at Tammy and added, "If you were in my shoes, what would you try to teach him?"

Tammy finished the last of her meal and sat back in her chair, considering the question. "First of all, you're great with people. You're such an encourager when you talk to them. You have a unique way of making people feel better about themselves, or the situation they're in, when you finish a conversation with them. Even when people don't agree with you, they respect your honesty. Just teach him that. Have him follow you around for a day and observe the master at work."

Bill laughed, setting his fork down on the remains of his salad. "The master?" he joked. "I already gave you your review and pay increase for the year. What else do you want?"

Leaning forward and folding her arms on the table, looking hard into Bill's eyes, Tammy replied, "Bill, I meant everything I said. You're great with people. If anyone can get Randy to open his eyes, it's you."

Bill smiled. "Thanks for your faith in me. Can you tell Randy all those things?" They both laughed. "Seriously, though, I need to be able to verbalize his behaviors in a way so that they are not mere words on a sheet of paper. I need him to feel them and be compelled to change his behavior. I need to get him to *feel* the problem." Waving to the waiter, he added, "Let's get the check and get back to the office." They stood up from the table, paid the bill, and headed out to the car.

As they drove, they discussed the situation further, and Bill found he was feeling better about the task at hand. His conversation with Tammy had spurred some ideas. The two said their goodbyes, and Bill headed back to his office.

Looking at his watch, he could not believe it was already 1:30 p.m. He thought to himself, *Crocoll, you better be good under pressure, because you have just three and half hours to get this plan together. Just write; don't evaluate the ideas to death, just write.* He began to list everything he knew about people. Rubbing his head, he leaned back in his chair and tried to categorize his thoughts; when he was finished writing, he had at least eight buckets of concepts. A sense of hope began to seep into his mind that maybe, just maybe, he could get through to Randy.

Bill stood up from his chair and stretched his arms. "I need to think outside the box," he said out loud. "How do I convey these messages about people in a way that will open Randy's eyes?" He opened a document on his PC and titled it "Eight Essentials of People." Eight bullet points later, he found himself talking out loud again. "I've got everything I know about people in eight short concepts, but now how do I make them come alive?" As he continued pondering his list, more ideas came to mind, lessons from past victories and failures. He thought of the real-life experiences he had gone through in his own journey, and the stories of his friend's experiences. He was reminded of the help and encouragement he had received from effective leaders during the development of his career. The more he thought and wrote, the more excited he became about the plan, especially the process of relaying the concepts to Randy. He knew this could work, though he wasn't sure what Steve was going to think. He completed the list as the clock hit 4:55 p.m. *Nothing like waiting until the last minute,* he thought, but he was relieved that he had a plan. He printed the document and headed to Steve's office.

He arrived at Steve's office slightly out of breath. The door was open and Steve waved him in, finishing up a phone conversation. He could tell immediately that Steve was talking to Tom Karnes, his boss, explaining that a plan was nearly in place to address the issue with Randy, and that he was confident that Randy would be a success. Steve ended his phone call with Tom and turned his attention to Bill.

Steve stood up with a smile on his face, though a nervous one, shook Bill's hand, and asked, "Well, partner, do you have a plan to change Mr. Sysol's behavior? As you may have just heard, I've made a commitment to Tom that we'll make Randy successful. Do you have the cure, Dr. Crocoll?"

Bill was a little irritated with Steve's promise to Tom Karnes. How could Steve make a commitment like that without even having seen his plan? But he put his concerns aside and handed Steve the document he'd just printed. "You're going to have to trust me on this."

Steve quickly read through the plan, shaking his head several times, and sighing twice. Bill could tell he was not excited about what he was reading.

Steve took a deep breath and said, very seriously, "You've had all day to come up with a plan, and this is it? I don't know what it means. I'm under the gun from the president and my boss, and all you give me is this list of enigmatic phrases that have zero meaning to me. How am I going to explain this to Tom if I haven't got a clue what it means? What do 'M&Ms, *The Wizard of Oz,* Fishing Lures, Milk Bones, Rosetta Stone, (S + A = B) = O, Twenty Dollar Bill, and Green Beans have to do with Randy? With all due respect Bill, did you leave your mind in Ontario?"

Bill chuckled. "Steve, you've known me for a long time, and I can't think of a time that I've let you down. I know this is important to you, but remember that my reputation and neck are on the line, too. If you'll trust me and give me four weeks, I believe this plan will turn Randy around."

Steve raised his voice slightly. "I do trust you, but trust isn't the issue here. I need to understand the plan. This thing makes zero sense to me." Bill tried to respond, but Steve raised his hand to stop him. "How do I explain it to my boss? I know you've always come through for me in the past, but Bill, even the Mighty Casey struck out."

Bill leaned forward in his chair, looked directly into Steve's eyes, and said, "It may not make sense yet, but when we are done, you will see the beauty of it. This plan will touch his heart, and once we get his heart, his mind will follow. If you want me to go over the plan with you, I can, but I'm not sure it will make you any more confident in it. I can spend the next three or four hours reviewing it with you, or I can use that time to get to work. Four weeks is all I'm asking."

Steve got up from his chair and walked to the window. Gazing out at the sky, and without looking at Bill, he said, "I don't feel good about this, but I do trust your expertise. You can have the four weeks, but I'm going to need a weekly update on the progress of the plan. Agreed?"

Mark J. Balzer

"Agreed," said Bill with a smile.

As the two men shook hands, Steve sighed, "I'm banking my career on M&Ms and the Tin Man. I need my head examined."

Chapter Four
M&Ms

As Bill got dressed for work the next morning, his mind was occupied with the coming meeting with Randy. He headed down the stairs still musing, and almost walked right by his bag of M&Ms and candy dish on the kitchen counter as he said good morning to his wife Casey. His wife responded with a perplexed smile and a puzzled look on her face. "What in the world have you got there? Halloween isn't for a few months. And bribing employees with candy seems a little below you, honey."

Casey's response did not surprise him; her lighthearted banter was one of her most endearing traits. "It's not for bribing employees, it's to assist in training people skills into our new college hire ." He smiled playfully. "Sweetheart, I don't have time to explain it now, but I promise I'll fill you in later."

He grabbed the candy along with the other supplies for his plan, gave Casey a kiss, and headed toward the door. As he opened the door, he turned back to Casey and said, "I'll see you at 7:00 tonight. I love you."

Casey held up her right hand up in a gesture to draw his attention and said, "I love you too; remember, Ralston has a game tonight."

Bill remembered and was looking forward it; he always tried to make it to all the games he could. He assured her, "I know, and I'll be home in time for us to go together." He headed out the door, threw his props in the back seat, and drove off to work.

On his way to the office, thoughts of his first meeting with Randy were at the forefront of his mind. The plan was good; now the implementation needed to measure up. This was a critical stage for Randy's career, and Bill knew he needed to help Randy change his behavior before he dug himself any deeper. Turning the corner onto Washington Avenue, he saw Steve talking to a young man outside the facility. *That must be Mr. Sysol,* he thought. *He looks like a nice enough young man. I hope Steve isn't overselling the development plan.* He knew that Steve had a habit of downplaying the issues with a project, while playing up the results. But Randy's expectations needed to be managed appropriately. *I don't want him to think I have some magic pixy dust I can sprinkle on him and everything will be fixed,* Bill thought. *It's going to take time. I can't just give him my knowledge; he has to reach some conclusions by himself. Talking's the easy part; generating change is the challenge.* Entering the garage, he found an empty parking space up front. Bill smiled. *Great start to the day. I can't remember the last time I was able to park this close to the door. Hopefully this is a sign that my meeting with Randy will go well.*

Bill hurried into his office, dumped the M&Ms into the candy dish, and strategically placed it in a visible place on his desk. As he opened the window shades to let the sun in, the phone rang and he was notified that Randy Sysol was there to see him. Bill took a deep breath and actually said out loud, "Show time."

Sitting outside his office was the same young man he had seen talking to Steve in the parking lot. "You must be Randy Sysol," he said, shaking hands with him. "Come on in and have a seat, and we can get started." Bill held up his cup of coffee asked, "Would you like some coffee?"

Randy set his notebook down on his desk and responded, "No, sir. I'm hyper enough without caffeine. Besides, I'm a little nervous, and with my luck I'd probably spill it on your desk."

Bill was impressed both with Randy's dress and the way he addressed him as "sir." He could tell the young man was nervous, but could see nonetheless that Randy had an aura of confidence, and not the arrogance that he anticipated. Bill's initial impression was not what he expected, based on his conversations with Steve and Tammy. He was expecting a brash young man with attitude. Overall, his first impression was positive, and he was puzzled that Randy was unable to translate this behavior to his employees.

Bill opened the journal that contained his plan, and, leaning back in his chair, began speaking. "First of all Randy, please call me Bill. 'Sir' sounds like my father, and I'm not that old yet. Second, there's absolutely nothing to be nervous about. I thought we could spend a few hours together and get to know each other. I'm very excited about the opportunity to work with you over the next few weeks, and I hope we can both grow from the experience. I've been here for over ten years and if you have any questions or concerns, I'm here to help you. How does that sound?"

Randy had unconsciously perched anxiously on the edge of his seat. He noticed his posture and instantly slid back and let out a slight chuckle. "Wow. That's a relief. When Steve told me I would be meeting with the manager of human resources to discuss my performance, the first thing I thought was, this can't be a good thing. I thought you were meeting with me to fire me. Glad I was wrong."

The relief was visible in Randy's expression as he continued, "I asked Steve what the purpose of the meeting was, but he was very vague. He told me I would find out in the morning from you. You can probably tell, I didn't sleep very well last night, thinking about it."

Bill shook his head, smiling. "I'm not sure why HR has the reputation of being the hatchet people. People think HR reps keep body bags in their briefcases. I can assure you that this is not the case here. I see myself as a business leader who happens to work in HR. We don't hire people to fire people; we hire people to make them successful. Anyway, sorry about the stress this meeting has caused you, Randy. I want you to know that my job is to make all of our leaders at Dunkirk successful. Steve thought it would be a good idea if you and I worked together for a few weeks to ensure you have a resource to reach out to if you need it. Are you ready to get started?"

Randy had relaxed considerably, but he wanted to make sure not to drop his guard. He didn't want to be too confident and miss any signs. There had to be some reason for this meeting. He asked, "Before we get started, can I ask one question? Why haven't I met you before? I started two months ago. I've heard your name several times from members of the staff and my team, but I've never seen you in the building. I heard you were working on a start-up somewhere, but not ever meeting you, and then suddenly a formal appointment -- I admit, that's part of what had me worried."

Bill could sense Randy was still a little on edge. "I was working on a start-up in Ontario, California, providing HR support for one of our biggest customers," he explained. "We were having issues with the hiring and on-boarding process and they needed an extra set of hands. It was nothing special, just basic blocking and tackling. Really, the only problem was with my family. It wasn't just my being away for two months; we had a vacation planned to visit Hawaii, and we had to cancel the trip. We were going to celebrate our twenty-fifth wedding anniversary there. That didn't go over well with her or my kids. If I hadn't been working on the start-up, I would have met you on day one. I usually make it a point to meet everyone on their first day, to welcome them to Dunkirk Distribution. I wish Steve would have explained my absence."

This made sense to Randy. He relaxed a bit more and responded, "I hope down the road some time, I get the opportunity to work on a start-up with Globalistics. Erin Bryum, my counterpart at second shift, told me they were very rewarding. She said they're a lot of hard work, but you also have the opportunity to set up the culture the right way from the beginning, leave your finger prints on the site."

Randy paused for a split second, thinking about how difficult it must have been for Bill to tell his family their trip would have to be postponed. He went on, "I can see why your wife and kids were upset, though. Man, Hawaii would be amazing to visit; it's a dream of mine to go there. I grew up in Iowa, and I've never even seen the ocean. My apartment here is right on Lake Erie, though. The lake looks huge, so I can only imagine how big an ocean is." Randy paused, "Oh yeah, and congratulations on twenty-five years. I've been seeing someone for two years, and that seems long. I can't imagine being with the same person for twenty-five."

Bill laughed and took a sip of his coffee. "I definitely got the better end of the deal. She's the most amazing person I've ever met. Without her support and encouragement, I'm not sure where I'd be today. She's a great wife and a great mother to my three kids. She's our glue. " Bill handed a picture of his family to Randy and went on. "I'm sure one day you'll have a chance to work on a start-up, and a chance to visit Hawaii. And yes, and the ocean is much bigger than Lake Erie."

Both men laughed as Bill took out a pad of paper and a copy of Randy's resume. "Your background's very impressive, Randy. You've accomplished a lot for someone your age. Could you walk me through your life's history? Your childhood in Iowa and move to New York; your family, education, work experience, and anything else you'd like to share about yourself?"

Randy made himself comfortable in the chair and crossed his legs. "Sounds like the beginning of another interview to me," he said good-naturedly.

Bill picked up his pen and wrote at the top of a page in his journal, "Meeting one," and then gestured for Randy to continue, saying, "Nah, I'd just like some background information to help me get to know you better. When you're done, I'll tell you all the same stuff about myself, or anything else you'd like to know about me. You can drill me. My life is an open book."

Randy was entirely relaxed now. "Sounds good to me Bill, although I'm not sure how exciting it will be for you. I was born and raised on a farm in Osceola, Iowa. It's a small town about an hour south of Des Moines. The farm has been in my dad's family since the early 1900s. It was a great life if you like the outdoors, especially if you like to hunt. I loved getting up early in the morning, heading to the woods before the sun came out. It was so peaceful and relaxing. It was a great way to clear your mind and think about life. I wish I could make a living at it."

Bill politely interrupted, "Not much of a hunter myself, but I sure love to fish. Nothing more relaxing than sitting back, enjoying the sun, and catching a few; my fishing is like your hunting."

Randy nodded in agreement. "You'll have to give me some fishing tips sometime." He went on enthusiastically, "I loved growing up in the country and living on a farm. I love the smell and sound of the country. There's nothing like it. The air is clean, and the noise of the farm is actually very calming, being able to walk around without anyone bothering you. I miss it, just talking about it."

Bill could see the contentment in Randy's eyes as he talked about his home life. "Randy, it sounds wonderful. I'm surprised you didn't go back to your family's farm."

Randy nodded again. "That part of living in the country I loved, but there are parts I didn't like at all. I didn't enjoy bailing hay in the summer time. A hundred degrees out in the field, and we'd work from sunrise to sunset seven days a week. You end up too tired to do anything at night."

Randy remembered thinking that his parents must have loved the busy part of the summer, because the kids were so tired from working all day they would come home early and go straight to bed. Laughing, he explained to Bill, "My parents enjoyed that aspect of hay season. They knew their kids would be home early at night. I'm very proud of my mom and dad and the life they provided for me, but I knew farming was not what I wanted to do for the rest of my life. I love the country life, the wide open space and fresh air, but not the farming part. I truly admire my mom and dad for their commitment to their work and instilling me with a strong work ethic. "

He paused, reminiscing. Then he went on, "Honestly, that was my motivation to excel and apply myself in school. I knew school was my ticket off the farm."

Bill took another sip of his coffee and wiped his hand across his forehead. "A hundred degrees bailing hay . . . that would motivate me to get out of farming, too; I really don't enjoy hot, hot weather. So, farming is out, but with all the career possibilities one could pursue, why did you choose distribution? It is not the sexiest career choice."

Randy was gaining confidence as the conversation continued . "I was always interested in how our crops got to market and onto people's tables. My family's farm was just one of thousands of farms across the country. I thought it was fascinating how the huge quantity of crops grown in our area were transported all over the country." He went on, "I had an uncle that worked as a forklift driver at a local food distributor; he gave me a tour of the place he worked at, and it was awesome. Everything was highly automated, and the warehouse management system was incredible. The facility had five miles of conveyors in it. I never realized the amount of specialized technology used in distribution. I began researching careers in distribution and logistics, and decided that was what I wanted to do with my life." He grinned. "Are you bored yet?"

Bill stopped writing in his journal and looked up. "Not at all, Randy. I always find it interesting, how and why people end up in their careers. Many people like you know early on what they want to do, but many others receive a degree and never end up using it. So some people come in to a company like this one through the front door; some people come in through the back. Me, I wanted to work with people, so I looked for a career involving leadership. Can't stand being chained to a chair all day; I need to interact with others. I think that's the important thing about your career. Find something you love that doesn't feel like work. Why did you choose Iowa State for college?"

"I was a small town kid and I wanted to stay close to home. I was accepted to Ohio State as well as the University of Tennessee. I loved both schools, but my heart was in Iowa. My family didn't travel much; all I've ever really known was Iowa, and the university's only about two hours away from where I grew up. I had an offer of an academic scholarship there; mom and dad didn't have much money, so economically it made sense. And, of course, their logistics and distribution program is outstanding.

"My GPA was 3.9," Randy added. "I had all As, except for one B in some silly interpersonal communication class. You know one of those 'touchy-feely' type classes. It was a degree requirement course, otherwise I wouldn't have taken it."

Bill rubbed his chin thoughtfully and leaned forward slightly. "Why did you think it was silly, Randy?"

Surprised, Randy answered, "The class had nothing to do with the real world, or with distribution. It was a waste of time and energy. I had to sit through two lectures and an hour lab each week and talk about basic, common-sense drivel. The exercises and experiments we were required to complete were useless. The liberal arts and theater majors ate it up, but I'm a numbers person. The instructor marked me down for class participation, but it's hard to participate in a class when you know it won't help you in your career. I had zero interest in any of it. You must have had classes that added nothing to your knowledge or skill base, right?"

Bill paused to take another sip of his coffee and nodded, but he was beginning to see the gap in Randy's thought process. Randy placed heavy emphasis on his technical expertise, but trivialized the people component of leadership. Bill thought, *Ducks. If it looks like a duck, and it talks like a duck, it's a duck. We do have a young Tim Bender here.* He just hoped that Randy's understanding of leadership as an equation made up of numbers and results wasn't as entrenched in his behavior as it had been in Bender's. "Randy, I think everyone has a class or two like your interpersonal communication course, but I would challenge your claim that it has no relationship to distribution."

Randy was startled; he wondered what interpersonal communication could have to do with a supply chain. Supply chain was all about moving freight and meeting customer orders. In his confusion, Randy found his thoughts drifting, so he focused his attention back on Bill, who was still speaking. "We can have that debate another time. Right now, I'd really like to know how you think you're doing here. What's going well? What are your challenges? Any issues or problems or questions that you have, let's discuss them."

Randy did not respond immediately; he was still a little distracted by Bill's previous comment, and was a bit uncomfortable with his current question. Feeling the silence, he knew he had to pull it together and give an honest answer. It had only been two months, and he knew there were still things he needed to learn; he also knew he was having some issues with associates in his department. What he did not know, was how much Bill knew about it. Bill, on the other hand, could see a change in Randy's facial expression; he looked nervous again, and he began to fidget in his chair.

His suspicions were confirmed when Randy hesitated, before saying, "Looks like it's time to get down to business." He took a deep breath. "I guess, pretty well so far. I understand the warehouse management system and the product flow in and out of the building. I recently changed the process for cycle counting, which increased our accuracy and productivity. I haven't heard any complaints. I'm only two months into my career here, but Jack O'Connor, my operations manager, has said that my knowledge of the warehouse management system is further along than most new supervisors'. I was really happy to hear that from him. Of course, there's a lot more to learn, but overall I think it's going well. "

"That's really good to hear, Randy. I know making the transition from the classroom to the workplace can be challenging. I struggled in my first job. I had the technical ability to perform well, but the people side was tough at first. Looking back, I'm not sure how I survived. My leadership ability was weak at best. I started out as a supervisor in distribution like you, and had people working for me who were twice my age." Randy's eyebrows registered his surprise that Bill had started out in operations. "I kept thinking, 'How am I going to relate to these people? We are from different generations, we see the world from completely different perspectives.' But after struggling for a while, things fell into place. You didn't mention anything about your team. How are your relationships with them going? Do you have any difficulty relating to them?"

Bill turned to the window and closed the blinds partially against the bright sun. By the look on Randy's face, Bill could see he had hit a nerve. Again, Randy paused before responding; it was obvious that Bill had been made aware of some of the challenges he had been facing. Randy knew he was having issues, but were they out of the ordinary; it was just that these people were set in their old ways. *As a supervisor, I have to make changes even if they are not comfortable with them.* Randy began to speak, nervously, but directly. "How am I relating to my people? Good question. Can I be upfront with you?"

Bill returned to his chair with a glass of water for Randy and closed his journal, so Randy could see that he had Bill's undivided attention. "Of course you can. If you and I are going to have a relationship, it has to be based on trust. If trust doesn't exist between people, then you don't really have a relationship." Bill paused to be sure Randy was understanding his message. "I want to assure you, I have your best interests at heart. I am here to help you be successful, not to pass judgment. Look at me like a coach." Bill leaned forward in his chair. "Please continue."

Randy felt his guard drop a bit; he really did need someone to trust. He had done very well in school, with all the projects and classes, but this was the real deal, and as hard as he tried, some things hadn't yet fallen into place. It had nothing to do with effort – something was just not clicking. Having someone to trust and confide in could make a difference. Randy thanked Bill for the water and decided to be open. "Actually, I'm not doing well at all with my people. Some of them are responding and doing what I need them to do. I think some of them hate me. Well, 'hate' is a strong word; they strongly dislike like me, at least for now. It's mostly the more tenured people. They are stuck in their ways. I don't understand why, either. I'm trying to teach old dogs new tricks. They just hate change. I guess."

Randy took a sip of water and continued, "Not that it matters that much. I don't get paid to be liked, I get paid to get things done. And I am getting things done, which is the important thing. I'm trying to make their job easier, not harder. We have a few weeks before our volume spike, and I'm trying to get our processes in line to handle it. I just don't understand why they can't see it. I've changed several processes, for the better, and you'd think I ran over their dog. Two people in particular gave me the hardest time about a change I made in one area; it was to the point that I had to give them a verbal warning to get on with the program. I have no idea what they want, need, or expect from me. The one thing you can count on, though, I'll get the job done, with or without them. And I think over time I'll win them over."

Bill kept his reactions in check as he listened to Randy, but he couldn't believe what he was hearing. He had been convinced Randy wouldn't have a realistic perspective about his relationship with his team. In fact, he had thought Randy would probably say his relationship with the team was good, and would be defensive to any feedback about his people skills. He thought the first battle would be to get Randy to recognize he had a problem. The good thing was that Randy knew there were issues in the relationship; in fact, he had a pretty realistic perspective. The bad thing was, he just didn't see it as a problem, so much as a temporary setback. This was a totally different issue. Bill didn't want to break the flow of the conversation; he wanted Randy to be as open as possible, so he nodded his head, encouraging Randy to continue.

Randy pulled out the roster of his team from the back of his notebook and said, "Part of the problem is all the different types of people on the team. There's the obvious age difference between me and most of my team, but I don't think that's the biggest problem I have with them. I've got people from Bosnia, Somalia, India, Canada, Korea, Mexico, Puerto Rico, African-Americans, people from the city, and of course a bunch of New Yorkers. And I'm just an old country boy from Iowa. We only had one type of person in our town: hard-working farmers, ninety-nine percent of them white. I'm having a hard time with the diversity, I think. There are so many different cultural backgrounds on the team, and I really don't have anything in common with them. We're from completely different worlds. I don't think I'll ever relate to some of them. To be honest, I don't have the time or energy to understand their culture; they need to adapt to our culture at Dunkirk. I figured that since I can't relate to them on a personal level, I'll earn their respect by showing them my expertise. I may be from Iowa, but I'm no country bumpkin when it comes to distribution. I know my way around a warehouse. Eventually, my team will appreciate that I know my stuff."

Bill saw an opportunity to implement the first of his topics. He knew he needed to be careful and not rush it. He also knew that Randy was missing an important part of leadership, and he needed to maintain his trust to point it out to him. So Bill started with a simple question. "Randy, how is your plan working for you so far?"

Randy's head tilted slightly, and he asked in a guarded tone, "What do you mean, how is my plan working? We're meeting the productivity numbers on my shift, so it looks like the plan is working just fine!"

Bill smiled, to ease the growing tension. "Are you getting the results you want from your team? Are you meeting the needs of the business, and the needs of your team?"

Randy fidgeted with his notebook took a deep breath. "From a technical perspective, I wouldn't change a thing. In the two months since I started here we have had small improvements in all our KPI's. I know Steve's noticed; he mentioned the KPI improvements to me this morning. The people side is a little bumpy right now, but with time, they'll see that their jobs are becoming easier with the changes I've made, and they'll come around. I will admit, their reluctance to accept change is frustrating right now, but nobody likes change, right? Most of my team have been with the company for several years, and they're just resistant to anything that disrupts the way they've always done things. I understand why they don't like changing, but we can't be stuck in the past! We need to constantly challenge the process."

Randy paused for a moment. He could tell that the pace of his answer was fast and had a defensive air to it. He didn't feel threatened by Bill's question; he simply didn't understand why his team was so resistant, and he didn't want it to appear that he didn't have control of the situation. He leaned back in his chair and continued, "Any suggestions on how I can speed up their acceptance of these changes? I need to accelerate this, before I'm forced to write-up some senior employees. I'd hate to take that course of action, but I'm not afraid of it, either. If we think outside of the box, we can improve the business."

Bill knew the conversation was at a critical juncture; in building trust with Randy, he needed to proceed with caution. This young man had been successful throughout his entire life, and now he was facing his first major problem two months into his career, and he had no idea of the magnitude of it. Matter of fact, Bill wasn't even sure Randy thought he had a problem. In Randy's mind, he was doing what he was getting paid to do: hitting the KPI's. Bill knew he needed to talk to Steve and Jack about what they were reinforcing to Randy about the importance of the numbers. They were making his task much harder by focusing only on productivity with him, and not people. Leadership is a balance of productivity and people, and Bill knew that if you get the people part wrong, the productivity side won't matter.

"Randy, before I start offering any suggestions to you, I'd like to ask a few more questions, to better understand the complete picture. Is that okay with you?"

Randy felt like he had shared as much as he could, if not too much, already. He appreciated the fact that Bill was interested in his situation, but he did not know what else he could say. He answered with a hint of frustration in his tone, "I guess so, but I'm not sure if I have much more to add to the story. The business needs are being met, and some people need to be corrected. It doesn't take a brain surgeon to figure it out; some people just don't like change."

"Fair enough, Randy. We can discuss your first few months in more detail later, but right now let's move on." Bill reached for his journal, glanced over the list of questions he had prepared, and said, "My first question for you is, what is your leadership purpose?"

"What is my leadership purpose? Hmm. Could you be a little more specific? I'm not sure what you mean by 'leadership purpose'."

Bill sensed Randy was tensing up, so he kept his voice calm as he responded, "Sure thing: why did you want to become a leader? Why not just be an individual contributor? Why did you want the challenge of leading other people? Does that clarify my question?"

"Yeah, I think I got it." Randy appeared to be thrown off by Bill's question. "Gosh, I'm not sure. Never really gave it much thought. Honestly, is it really that important to know your *leadership* purpose? I come into work every day with a work purpose for the associates and myself. Actually, I have a to-do list that helps me stay on track, and get through the work load Steve requires each day."

Bill could see that Randy had confused organization and being busy with leadership; Randy's tone and the response to Bill's question gave him even clearer insight into the attitude Randy took when his work behavior was questioned. *Is it really that important? Is he serious?* Bill wanted to set the record straight with Randy in no uncertain terms, but knew better than to be that direct at this stage of the process. He took a deep breath and responded, "Yes, Randy, I do think knowing your leadership purpose is important. Whatever your leadership purpose is will define your leadership behavior. I know my leadership purpose has shaped the way I behave when I lead others. I do not question your work ethic, and I know there are times when leaders think that being organized and busy amounts to quality leadership. It's a part of leadership, but it cannot replace or produce the long-term results of a leadership purpose."

Randy found himself on the edge of his seat again. *Why am I feeling so defensive?* he thought. *Bill's not attacking me, yet I feel like I have to defend my way of getting things done. I guess it's obvious that I'm having some issues with directing my team.* With a degree of hesitation in his voice, Randy said, "Bill, let me ask you a quick question, or maybe it is an observation. You and I come from two different worlds and generations. With all due respect, perhaps when you attended college and started your career, knowing your 'leadership purpose' was important, but things are different today. The business world is more sophisticated and complex than ever before. I took plenty of business classes in college, and I was never asked what my leadership purpose is. My instructors focused on real business needs and challenges. We did case study after case study to understand the financial pressures on businesses and their bottom line. It was about business trends and numbers and results, not leadership philosophy. "

Bill immediately recalled his conversations with Steve and Tammy about Randy's phrase "old school." "So do you think knowing your leadership purpose is old-school thinking?"

"I hate to say it, but yes." Randy paused for a few seconds to see if Bill was going to respond before he continued, "It sounds like old school thinking to me. We can discuss the philosophical aspects of leadership if you want, but at the end of the day, it's about results. Again, please don't take my comments as being disrespectful, but you asked for honesty, and I want to be fair to both of us by being open."

Self control, Bill told himself, *Self control, self control. Put things in perspective.* Randy was young and needed to open his eyes and think outside his own experience. "I appreciate your honesty and I know you are not being disrespectful. I asked for honesty and you're being honest. It's refreshing when someone doesn't pull any punches and is straightforward. It's a good trait to have, and I respect that characteristic in people."

Randy could feel his guard dropping again; it was like a see-saw, up and down, up and down. He took a sip of his water and explained, "I was raised with those values. My father's favorite saying was 'say what you mean and mean what you say.' If you ask me my opinion, I will give it to you. You might not always like it or agree with it, but it will be honest."

Bill could feel himself calming down. He had to remind himself that this was not just an issue for young college graduates; he dealt with individuals of all ages who balked at the importance of a leadership purpose. So Bill replied, "I agree with your father's philosophy. I'll have to remember that saying. Do you mind if I use it in my training classes? I'll be sure I give your father the credit."

Randy half-way smiled and replied, "You sure can, and you don't need to give my dad credit. I doubt he's the originator of the saying anyway."

Acknowledging Randy's straightforwardness seemed to have broken some of the tension in the room. Bill shifted the subject again. "Randy, I came across something interesting the other day in a book I'm reading. It was a quotation: 'If you want to test a man's character, give him power.' What do you think?. Do you agree with the quote, or not?"

Bill was surprised by Randy's facial expression. Randy squirmed in his chair a little, and with slight increase in the pitch of his voice, answered, "Bill, are you asking me what I think of the quote because you're questioning my character? If that's the case, I must take offense to your question. My character and integrity have never been questioned, ever. People might not always like or appreciate me, but they respect my character."

Bill made eye contact with Randy and said, "Hold on. If that's the way you interpreted my question, please accept my sincere apology. I can assure you that my question was in no way directed at your character. I can tell by the little time we have spent together that you have a solid ethical foundation. I'm just wondering what you think about the quote I read. That's it."

Randy closed his eyes briefly before he responded. "I'm sorry about my reaction, but I believe if you don't have personal integrity, you don't have anything. I'll take feedback from anyone, but I need to protect who I am as a person."

"I agree with you about that. And, thinking about the way I phrased the question, I probably would have responded the same way you did. Are we good, Randy?"

Randy shook his head yes. "We're good. Now let me think about the quote for a minute." Randy uncrossed his arms as he thought. "Bill, the idea of character and power going together make sense; I can see how a person with power has the ability to use it for good or harm. I believe a leader should be held accountable for their use of the power given to them. Going back to my father, he's a man of great integrity, and has never bullied anyone. People who are given power need to use it appropriately and not abuse it. I suppose it does test your character at some level."

Bill could see by Randy's gestures and response that he had taken the quote to heart. He asked, "Do you think the quote is timely? Can it apply to the issues you and I deal with daily?"

Randy nodded. "Yes, it definitely can apply today; it would be applicable to any of us. The fact that any leader is constantly in a position of influence, whether positive or negative, confirms that it applies today."

"Do you know the author of that quote? Think about it for a minute while I stretch my legs. I hurt my knee playing softball before I went to California, and every once in a while it stiffens up on me." Bill stood up and began to walk back and forth behind his desk.

Randy thought for a moment as Bill continued pacing. "I haven't a clue who said that. Wait a minute, is it Steven Covey?"

"No, it isn't Covey, but I could see him saying something along those lines." Bill reached in this desk and pulled out Covey's book *The Eighth Habit*. "I've read most of Covey's stuff; this book especially is fantastic." Randy didn't respond to his comment about the book, so he went back to his earlier question. "The author of the quote is Abraham Lincoln. Do you think Lincoln is old school?"

Randy smiled and looked down at the floor. "Okay, I can see where you're going with this. I concede; you got me on this one. Lincoln was probably our greatest president, and no, his quote isn't old school. The man was an amazing leader, but I'm shocked I didn't know Lincoln said that. I have read a lot about Lincoln."

Still on his feet, Bill agreed, "Lincoln was a great leader and I believe, also, that he was our greatest president. The point I am trying to make to you is that some leadership principles are timeless. Don't you agree?"

"Yes, I agree that some principles have withstood the test of time."

Bill smiled. "So, back to my question, what is your leadership purpose? For the sake of argument, let's just say my question is not old school, and that it is a leadership principle that is timeless. Can you go along with me on this one?"

Randy sat back in his chair. "Sure, why not, it's a timeless principle. Now why should I spend time figuring out what my leadership purpose is? I'm not trying to be smart with you, but I just can't get my mind around the concept."

Bill sat back down at his desk and asked, "For instance, if a person's leadership purpose is to make more money, what do you think drives their day-to-day behavior?"

"If a person got in to leadership just to make more money, they probably focus their daily behavior on results."

"Why on results, Randy?"

Randy looked down at the floor and then back up at Bill, and responded, "If money is their purpose, then they need to get results so they can get a larger merit increase or be promoted to the next level."

Bill nodded and said, "Right on, Randy. They would want to make more money, and to make more money, they would need results at all costs. Their focus would not be on their people's needs, but on the business's needs. Where is the respect for others in their leadership equation?" Bill stopped momentarily to let Randy digest the concept and then he continued. "These people do not understand that people-orientation and task-orientation are not either-or possibilities. You can meet the needs of the business and at the same time meet the needs of the people. Do you think their leadership purpose drives their behavior?"

Before he responded to Bill, Randy wrote "Leadership purpose" in his notebook. "I see your point, Bill; their purpose for getting into leadership would drive their behavior."

"Let me ask you, then, is knowing your leadership purpose important?"

Randy smiled and said, "Why do I have this feeling you've tricked me into agreeing with your premise?"

Bill laughed. "Randy, I wasn't trying to trick you at all. I just wanted to get you to think outside the box. You still haven't answered my question, though. As a leader, is it important that you know your leadership purpose?"

Randy put his hands in the air, signaling his surrender. "Okay, you win. Knowing your leadership purpose is important. Before you ask me this question again, I really do not know what my leadership purpose is right now. I can give you a canned response, but I would prefer a day or two to think about it. Is that okay with you?"

"That would be perfect. I want you to give that question some thought. You should do some real soul-searching. You need to know what drives your behavior." Bill felt he had had a minor breakthrough with Randy and wanted to push his agenda forward. "Are you ready for my next question, Randy?"

"I know you said I would be given time to ask you questions when we got done with my interrogation." Randy looked at Bill for a reaction to his comment, but Bill appeared impassive. "Just kidding, Bill. Can I ask you a quick question?"

Bill responded confidently, "Absolutely. Ask away, Randy."

"What is your leadership purpose?" Randy picked up his pen, preparing to write down Bill's response.

"You get right to the point, don't you? It's pretty simple and straightforward. My leadership purpose is to help people that cannot help themselves." Randy didn't immediately respond, and Bill could tell Randy was hesitant to comment on Bill's purpose. "You look puzzled. What do you think of my leadership purpose? Don't lose your candor now. Out with whatever you're thinking, Randy."

Randy looked around the room and explained, "Your purpose sounds more like a social worker statement than a leadership purpose. I don't get it at all. People get paid to do a job. We're not their keepers; people need to take responsibility for themselves. If they can't help themselves, then why are they even on your team?"

"Let me explain my leadership purpose in more detail. This may take a few minutes, if that's okay with you." Randy nodded. "Randy, I grew up on the other side of the tracks in Dunkirk. My parents were very hard-working people, but they didn't make very much money. We always had our needs taken care of, but rarely any of our wants. When I was sixteen years old, I applied and got a job with the city. My summer was spent hacking weeds by hand on the railroad track on Third Street. Do you know the tracks I'm talking about?"

Randy pointed to the window in Bill's office and said, "I know where the tracks are. They run the entire length of the street. Doesn't sound like a great job."

"It wasn't a great job at all, but I needed the money." Bill shook his head. "We didn't have weed whackers back then; we used a sickle. Using a sickle's pretty old school, right?"

Both men laughed and Randy agreed, "Right. Using a sickle is definitely old school. How old are you?"

"Easy there, Randy, I'm not that old. It was 1977. We worked eight hours a day with a ten minute break in the morning and afternoon, and a twenty minute lunch break. It was a humid summer and our boss didn't allow extra water breaks. I had blisters on top of blisters and poison ivy from the top of head to the tips of my toes."

"It sounds as bad as baling hay in Iowa. You must have hated it."

"Not sure if it was as bad as baling hay, but it was bad. The one aspect of my summer job that was probably worse than yours, though: you worked for a person that cared about your well being, and I didn't. Our boss was a miserable person that treated us like we were dirt. The words 'please' and 'thank you' were not in his vocabulary. We were just trash to him, and there wasn't anything we could do about it. We didn't have anybody we could talk to about him. During that summer, I made a commitment to myself. Someday I was going to be a boss, and I was going to fight for the underdog. I would help people that couldn't help themselves. I know it's a long explanation, perhaps a little sappy, but that's why I have the leadership purpose I do."

Randy lowered his head before responding. "I'm sorry about the social worker thing, Bill. I understand what it means now. I've heard a lot of employees talk about you on the floor, and how much they respect you. I thought it was because you were some touchy-feely HR guy that probably caved into all of their complaints. But they respect you because you're there for them when no one else will listen to their concerns. That's pretty cool."

Bill smiled and replied humbly, "Thanks for the compliment. I try to live my purpose daily, and I've connected with all of the people on the floor. I know not everyone likes me, but I think most people respect me." Bill pointed to a file cabinet in the corner and added, "That's where I keep all the corrective action notices. I'm sure some of those people wouldn't speak so highly of me."

Randy nodded his head and said, "Bill, I don't think you need to worry; most people do respect you. To be honest, I've never heard anything bad about you."

Bill laughed and replied, "That's because you have only been here for a couple of months. Give it some time, and you'll hear some negative stuff. You can't make everyone happy. Anyway, I answered your question, so can we return to your 'interrogation'?"

Randy said, apologetically, "I'm sorry about that comment as well, Bill. I was trying to be funny."

Bill laughed out loud and leaned back into his chair. Then he replied cheerfully, "Interrogation? I'll give you interrogation. Okay, Randy, let's get back to your first few months here. You said something that really stood out to me, and it was a strong statement. I want to understand your point of view on this. You said: 'The business needs are being met, and some people need to be corrected. It doesn't take a brain surgeon to figure it out; some people just don't like change.' Do you remember saying that?"

The question caught Randy off guard. Was this going back to the character and power quote again? "I remember saying it, and I stand by it. Some of these people have worked here for so long that they're just stuck in their ways. Yeah, I'm rocking their boat, but if they would get their heads out of the sand and take a look at the improvements I've made here, they would appreciate my effort instead of criticizing it. I'm not sure it's my problem. No, actually I am sure about this: it's their problem, not mine."

Bill could tell he had hit a nerve, so he shifted the conversation in a different direction. "What do you expect from Dunkirk Distribution? What do you want from the company?"

Randy moved in his chair and replied, a little tensely, "I'm not sure what you mean again. What do I want and expect from Dunkirk Distribution?" Shaking his head, he went on, "The question seems to imply that I'm doing something wrong here; if so, that's just not the case. Bottom line, my team is hitting their numbers. With all due respect, what I want and expect from Dunkirk Distribution is not going to help me get my people to accept change. I hope we're not going to make *their* problem into a Randy issue. Like I said, we're getting things done, and the team will come around. They just need some time to see the benefits of my changes."

Bill smiled, trying to reassure Randy that he was there to help him, and said calmly, "Randy, making the transition from the college classroom to the workplace has many challenges, and I'm here to help you with that transition, not to make anything a Randy issue." He paused briefly, allowing Randy to consider his comment. "The purpose of my question is to give us a frame of reference to discuss how we can speed up your team's acceptance of your changes. That's it. Your operation numbers are very good, but my question doesn't pertain to performance; it's about expectations. So, getting back to my question, what do you expect from Dunkirk Distribution? What do you want?"

Randy appeared to be a little more relaxed. "I want to move up in the organization, and I expect the organization to develop me in my profession."

Bill waited for a few seconds and asked, "Is that it?"

Randy again looked agitated. "What else is there? My goal is to become a general manager by the time I'm thirty years old, and I want Globalistics to provide me with developmental opportunities to reach my goal. Am I missing something, Bill?"

Bill said, shaking his head, "No, no, that's a great goal to have, and you realize you need to be developed to reach it." Bill paused for a moment, fiddling with the stress ball on his desk. "Randy, on a day-to-day basis, what will you need to do to reach your goal?"

Randy was doing his best to keep an open attitude towards Bill's questions. It was more difficult than he thought it would be. *It doesn't seem like he's out to get me,* he thought, but the questions made him uncomfortable and he couldn't quite figure out why. "Good question, Bill." Randy finished his water. "I'll need to apply my education, gain the respect of my peers, as well as senior management; make my numbers, provide a safe work environment, and continuously look for ways to improve the operation."

Bill wrote a few things in his journal, then looked back up at Randy. "Randy, what about the people on your team? Where do they fit in with your goal?"

Randy responded confidently, knowing he had to meet the expectations of the company with each associate in his department. "They need to do their jobs. I met with each person when I started and reviewed the standards for their job; I explained that I'll hold them accountable for meeting their numbers. Those who meet the standard get an incentive pay-out, while those who don't are written up. Pretty simple stuff – like I said, it's not rocket science."

"I see," Bill said, rubbing his chin. "Have you ever given this any thought: what do you think the people on your team want and expect from Dunkirk Distribution?" Bill was hoping this would be a breakthrough moment for Randy.

But to Bill's surprise, Randy answered the question very quickly and without much thought. "How would I know what they want from Dunkirk Distribution? We talk about what's best for the company; I can't meddle in their personal business, can I? I don't believe I'm responsible for figuring out their goals. People need to determine that for themselves." Randy could tell from Bill's facial expression that it was not the answer he was looking for. "I mean, I can help those that want to be helped, but their goals are their own. If the people on my team were truthful with us, they would say their goal at work is a paycheck. Their view of work is different from ours. We have a career. They have a job."

Bill leaned forward in his seat and looked directly into Randy's eyes and said, "You want the company to develop you, you want people to respect you, you want to learn new skills, you want to grow, and you want to get promoted to a general manager. Don't you think people on your team want some of the same things? Randy, don't you think it has to get deeper than a paycheck for them?"

"I don't know for sure. But if I had to guess, probably not. They're in a different job, with lower expectations. Like I said, hourly employees have jobs, not careers. It's a different perspective. Some members of my team have been here for years. If their goal is to move up, they haven't been very successful."

Bill realized he needed to change the direction of the conversation again. Randy's wall was up, and this line of questioning wasn't opening up Randy's mind. Bill picked up the dish of M&Ms and handed the dish to Randy. "Let's take a short break and have a few M&Ms."

Randy smiled. "I've been eyeing those things all morning. I love them."

Bill grabbed a handful of M&Ms and told Randy, "Good; have as many as you'd like. The more you eat, the less I do. I need to watch my waist." As Randy leaned forward to take a handful of M&Ms from the dish, Bill added, "By the way, what's your favorite color?"

Randy told him, "My favorite color is blue, but when it comes to M&Ms, I don't have a favorite color. I love them all!"

They both laughed as they ate their M&Ms. Bill sensed the mood in the room was lightening up, so he decided to go on with a few more questions. "So you don't have a favorite color of M&M. Why not?"

Randy looked at the M&Ms in his hand and noticed he had mostly red ones. He'd never really thought about a favorite color; he just liked eating them. A bit puzzled by the question, he answered, "I've never really thought about a favorite color of M&Ms. The way I see it, it doesn't really make a difference what color they are on the outside, because they're all the same on the inside. The color is just a coating over the chocolate." Randy bit off half of a yellow one and half of a red one, and displayed the leftover halves for Bill. "See? One's yellow and one's red, but it's all the same the inside. All chocolate, and all equally good."

Bill picked up another handful of M&Ms. "Good point, young man. Different colors of candy, but once you get past the outer shell, the M&Ms are all the same on the inside. Now, getting back to your team – you mentioned that you didn't feel like you were clicking with them. You're having problems relating to the different cultures they come from. You don't have anything in common with them. Is that correct?"

Randy really wanted to succeed with the team; he thought he just needed more time. "I think it may be an issue for me. I need to find some common ground. It will just take time."

Bill smiled and said, "Good, then, we're both on the same page. We need to find some common ground for you to build a relationship with your team. What would you say if I told you that actually, you have a lot of things in common with your team?"

One of Randy's eyebrows went up. "I would say that we're not on the same page at all. I believe we're very different, in that I'm open to change, and they resist it with a passion. Maybe you don't know my team, Bill."

Bill saw his opportunity to cover one of his principles of people leadership and went straight to the heart of the issue. "I know your team quite well. I have worked with several of them for years, and just as you do, I have many things in common with them." Randy tried to interject a comment but Bill put up his hand and continued with his thought. "People in my mind are just like M&Ms. The world is made up of many different colors of people, with different outer shells. We have black people, brown people, white people, red people, yellow people, and each type of people has a variety of shades. The reality is this: we're all the same on the inside. We all have a heart, lungs, ribs, stomach, intestines, etc. Do you really think you're different on the inside from Javier Lopez, Sebash Chardin,

Charlie Smith, or Henry Chu? The color of your skin may be different, your position in the company may be different, but on the inside, we're all the same, Randy."

Randy knew Bill was right, but could it be that easy – could human relationships be narrowed down to a handful of M&Ms? Randy wished it could be that easy, but looking at the different issues he was having with the team, he knew there was more to it. He told Bill, "Well, yeah, from that perspective I see your point, but how about different cultures?"

"Before we go any further, can we agree on the fact that people are all the same on the inside?" asked Bill.

"I will concede to that fact. On the inside, from a biological point of view, we're all the same."

"Good!" Bill said enthusiastically. "Sure, there are different cultures but let me share a story with you. A few years back I was invited to conduct a training class in Brazil. I was both excited and nervous about the opportunity. Admittedly, a lot of my anxiety about the training session had to do with immersing myself into their culture. How could I conduct a leadership class that was developed in North America to people from South America? I was afraid the program just wouldn't translate well; our culture and their culture were too different. I arrived in Sao Paulo, went outside of the airport, and saw the most amazing thing I'd ever seen. It blew me away. I'll always remember that moment, for the rest of my life. Do you know what it was?"

With a sense of excitement, Randy asked, "What was the most amazing sight you'd ever seen?"

"As I walked outside, I looked up at the sky, and . . ." Bill paused.

"And what?" Randy asked in anticipation.

"The sky, it . . . it was blue. With white clouds. When I looked around the city, they had cars, traffic lights, sidewalks, trucks, and people . . ." Randy began to smile, and let out a small laugh. "See, Randy, their world is just like ours. When people wake up in the morning in Brazil, they want to be respected just like the people in Osceola, Iowa. The United States doesn't have a monopoly on respect. All people want to be respected, valued, appreciated, developed, supported, recognized, and heard. Our cultures may be different, but people's needs are all the same with regard to respect. There are no favorite colors, only different colors among people; we're all the same on the inside. Javier, Subash, Henry, Charlie – they're not any different from you. When they wake up, they want to be respected, valued, developed, rewarded, and heard. Do you see my point?"

Randy responded sheepishly, "I'm trying to get your point. I can see the point you're trying to make, and it make perfect sense. I've never looked at it quite that way." He hesitated for a moment. "I guess people want those things from their manager. Looks like I might have missed the boat on this. I guess I do need to factor their development into my development. Where do I go from here?"

Bill let out an inward sigh; he was relieved to see that Randy was willing to be humble about his need to develop his leadership skills. Bill had one more thought he wanted to follow through with. "Let me ask you this before we talk about moving forward. When you where changing the processes in cycle counting, did you ask for any of your team's input prior to the change?"

Randy responded emphatically, "No, I . . . I didn't really think about their opinions. I just saw a way to improve it."

Bill interrupted Randy to ask," Do you think they felt valued and respected?" Before Randy could answer, Bill add another question. "When you were out there trying to impress them with your knowledge of distribution, did you give them a chance to impress you with their knowledge of distribution? Do you know Molly Fellinger has worked in this building for twenty-five years? She's worked here longer than you've been alive. Do you think she has some expertise about our business? Do you think she would like to feel important?"

Randy could feel the defensiveness building again; he was trying to be respectful. This idea of including the associates' input didn't make sense; it would simply open the door to chaos. Randy replied, though not as emphatically, "But Fellinger's not in charge. I'm responsible for making those types of decisions. I can't afford to make a mistake at this point in my career. My job is to make decisions, and her job is to implement my decisions."

Bill responded in a low tone, "Randy, I'm not saying you aren't responsible for making decisions, but put yourself in Molly's shoes for just a minute. Imagine you'd worked at Dunkirk Distribution for a quarter-century, and some twenty-two-year-old young man with two months of experience on the job comes in and starts changing things without asking what you think. Chances are, Molly would have seen the benefits of your proposed changes, but you didn't ask. How would it really make you feel?"

Randy looked down, feeling somewhat embarrassed by his behavior. "I'm starting to get your point. If I were in her shoes, I wouldn't like it either."

"Of course you wouldn't like it, but who would? If Steve Gugino made decisions for my HR team without consulting me first, I'd be livid. We all want to be valued and respected for our knowledge, skills, and experience. Trust me, your team members have goals just like you do. No disrespect to you and the other leaders at our facility, but the real experts in the building are our employees, not our leaders. Don't you think we should consider their experience and get their feedback before we implement changes here?"

All of Randy's defensive feelings had taken a backseat to the truth that Bill had just presented. He was beginning to see that it wasn't just about him; he had had a dismissive attitude and lack of respect toward "them." Even though it was an unintentional error, it still had the same negative setback for his team; people needed to feel valued. Randy could remember the times in his life when he hadn't felt valued, and he definitely remembered the people that had made him feel valued. Why did it take having this conversation with Bill to figure this out? With an entirely different attitude, Randy replied, "To be totally honest, I never looked at it that way. I wanted so much to impress people with my expertise that I didn't see how it was impacting others. I'm not usually a rude person, I try to be respectful of others, but I didn't see the big picture on this one. To answer your question, yes, I should seek their feedback on decisions that impact them."

Bill folded his hands on his desk and said, "I think you're right. Don't be too hard on yourself; many leaders fail to take advantage of the expertise of their people. I see so many leaders trying to solve problems without getting the true experts involved in the solution. Also when people have input into a decision they are more committed to the solution. But let's get back to our discussion about what you have in common with your people. Randy, you and the folks on your team aren't really so different on the inside, are you?"

Not really answering Bill's question, Randy went on, "Man, did I make a mess of things or what? I guess I didn't see the common ground between my team and myself. They're human just like I am, with the same basic needs. I really missed the big picture. I know if my boss treated me like that, I'd feel the same way they have. I'm beginning to see things much more clearly, why my team is not responding and relating to me. It's a lot more than their not liking change; it's my not relating to their needs. People are like M&Ms: all the same on the inside. I feel a little stupid right now."

Bill shook his head and responded gently, "Don't feel stupid. You can and will recover from this misstep. I went through the same thing when I first started out. The first thing we need to do is to help you see them as individual people, with legitimate needs; then we'll discuss their goals. Always remember this: before you became a leader, your development was all about you. Once you become a leader, you also become responsible for the development of your people. I want you to reach your goals, and you may be surprised to discover that if you lead them correctly, your team will want you to meet your goals as well. But they also have their own goals that they want to achieve. To reach their goals, they'll need your help. Does this make sense to you?"

Randy responded with a pained look on his face, "Yes, it does. I hate failing!"

"Whoa there, Randy – who said anything about failing? Not me. You haven't failed at all. We've identified an area for improvement, which is a good thing, my friend."

Randy let out a sigh. "I guess so. I just really missed the boat on this one."

Bill stood up and motioned Randy to join him at the window. "Look at this beautiful, sunny day. You know Randy, we wouldn't enjoy days like today if we didn't have cold, wet days, too."

Randy smiled. "That's true. If it never rained, you'd never appreciate the sunshine."

"Let's just say we've had a little rain at Dunkirk, but we have some bright days ahead. How about sitting down and developing an action plan for today, when you go down to the floor?"

"Let's do it!" Randy replied.

They two men returned to their chairs. For the next hour, they discussed and developed an action plan for Randy to establish credibility with his team. When they finished, Randy humbly thanked Bill for his time and his first lesson in people leadership: *People are like M&MS.*

"Before you go, Randy, I have an assignment for you. Have you ever seen *The Wizard of Oz?*"

Randy looked amused. "I saw it once, but it was ages ago. I remember some of the characters, but it wasn't one of my favorites. I'm more of an action-thriller type of guy. I love the technology and visual effects in modern movies. The older flicks just don't cut it for me. From what I remember, *The Wizard of Oz* was a very low-tech movie. Wasn't it made in the 50s?"

Bill laughed. "Actually, it was shot in 1939. Man, am I showing my age. It's my favorite movie of all time. When I was growing up, everyone loved the movie. It only came on once a year, though, as this was before DVDs or even videotapes, and the whole family always got together to watch it. It was a huge event. It brings back so many good memories. I have a copy of it here in my desk, and I want you to watch it tonight. Is that good with you?"

"Are you serious?" asked Randy.

"Yeah, indulge me; watch the movie tonight. We can talk about it tomorrow."

Randy looked down at the papers in the back of his notebook. "Bill, I'm not really sure I have time for that tonight, or this week. We're gearing up for peak season, so I'm putting in extra hours every night preparing for that. Tonight I have to cover for Harry, so I probably won't get home until midnight at least."

Bill looked at Randy and said, without missing a beat, "I know peak season is around the corner, and it's good you're getting ready for it. Let me ask you a question, though. What if I told you our meeting tomorrow is going to take place in Hawaii, and the flight leaves at 5:00 a.m.? You'll have to work until eleven o'clock, and after that you'll have to cancel your newspaper, have your mail held, and reschedule any appointments you have, cover the time off with your manager, go home and pack, and get some sleep. Can you be at the airport at 3:30 a.m. to check in for the flight?"

Randy responded enthusiastically, "If it were true, I'd be at the airport at 3:00 a.m.! I wouldn't miss a free trip to Hawaii. Are you kidding me? It would be outstanding!"

Bill nodded. "I'd be there too. You'd have to get a lot done in order to be there, but you'd make it. Do you know why you'd be there?"

Randy grinned. "Yeah, I'd get a free trip to Hawaii. Who wouldn't be there?"

Bill sat back in his chair and glanced at his journal. "Yes, it's a free trip to Hawaii, but the real reason you'd be there on time is that the trip to Hawaii is important to you. When things are important to people, they find time to get them done. If your development is important to you, then you'll find the time to watch the movie."

Randy couldn't believe he'd fallen for that one. Of course he could make the time to watch a movie; he simply didn't want to watch an old, boring one. But he also knew that he needed to improve his leadership skills, and if that meant watching a movie, then it looked like he'd be watching a movie. Randy said appreciatively, "It's important to me, so I'll watch it tonight. Thanks again for your help today; it really opened my eyes. I need to get down to the floor. See you tomorrow!"

Randy stood up and grabbed his notebook, and both men walked towards the door to Bill's office. They exchanged pleasantries and Randy headed out. Bill was extremely happy with the day's results; he felt they had made a major breakthrough.

Chapter Five
The Wizard of Oz

Bill arrived at his office at seven the next morning to prepare himself for his second meeting with Randy. He had to come up with a contingency plan, in case Randy had a setback on day one. Randy's buy-in to their first meeting was fragile, and if he'd reconsidered, they'd be back to square one. Randy just needed a few concrete successes to gain confidence, and the more success he had in dealing with his team, the more his commitment to Bill's coaching would grow.

Bill was writing down some key points to help Randy establish credibility with his people when his phone rang. He glanced at the caller ID; it was Steve. Bill hesitated; he didn't know if he should answer it or not. Maybe there had been another blow-up on the floor.

Bill picked up the phone. "Good morning, Steve. This is your humble HR manager Bill Crocoll; how can I help you?" Steve was all business, so Bill listened closely and then responded, "I have a few minutes this morning, but I need some office time to prepare myself for my meeting with Randy. I'll be right down, but I do want to stress that I only have a few minutes."

Bill began the long walk down to Steve's office, thinking that his plan needed time to work. *Rome wasn't built in a day. Developing people takes time, and people don't change overnight.* He could feel his frustration building as he thought of how behind he was, just having been gone for two months working on the start-up. He glanced at his watch, sighed, and opened the door. What he didn't need from Steve was any second guessing. The bottom line was that the first meeting had gone as well as could be expected.

"Mr. Gugino. What can I do for you, sir?"

" 'Mr. Gugino'? Wow, pretty formal today, aren't you? Please have a seat. I've got a few issues we need to discuss about the business, and I need an update on your progress with Randy. I was tied up all day yesterday in an off-site meeting, but I've been chomping at the bit wanting to find out how it went. With everything on my plate, I could really use some good news."

Steve went over several pressing issues the business was facing with the anticipated spike in volume at the building. When the hiring plan discussion was completed, Steve couldn't wait any longer. "So how did your meeting with Randy go yesterday? Don't hold anything back. Give it to me straight."

"It went extremely well. I can see now why Murphy is so set on his success. He has great potential. He just has a few wrinkles that need to be ironed out. He's very respectful and..."

Steve interrupted Bill mid-sentence. "Enough with the glowing appraisal; we both know his people skills are horrible. He's caused more damage on the floor in two months than most people cause in their entire career. I think he may have pulled the wool over your eyes like he did with Murphy. I don't buy into his country charm – the small kid from Iowa doing great in the big city. I have a folder in my desk full of complaints from the people that he's in charge of, so let's get to the point. What's his problem, and how are you going to fix it?"

Bill could feel himself growing angry, but he knew he had to hold it together. "Hold on, Steve. You asked me how the meeting went and I was telling you, until you interrupted. If you let me finish, I'll give you a blow-by-blow account. I'm not going to sugar coat anything. Now can I proceed?"

Steve, on the edge of his chair, knew he had crossed a line. "I'm sorry I interrupted you, and for my tone. This thing's really gotten under my skin. A day doesn't go by without my boss asking for an update. I can't believe the visibility this thing has higher up in the company. I have a building to run, a customer demanding perfection, the biggest volume projection in the history of this building coming in two weeks, unhappy employees, and the Sysol drama on top of it all. I'm just not myself today. Please do finish."

Bill, aware of the stress that came with the GM position, gave Steve a look of understanding. "Don't worry about it. I understand you're under a lot of pressure. As I was saying, he's a respectful young man, and wants to do the right thing as he sees it. He understands there are people problems with his team. That is a good sign. The bad news is that he doesn't see the problem as a major concern yet. His head is too wrapped around productivity and numbers, rather than around building relationships with his people."

Steve tried to interrupt. "That's what I —"

Bill said, "Hold on. He listened to what I had to say, and he seems committed to making some changes in his behavior. He has people skills; he just doesn't know how to apply them to his team. His approach was wrong from the beginning, and when things didn't go well, he tried to impress them rather than relate to them. I'm anxious to see how yesterday went for him. He left my office with a different perspective on people."

As Bill took a sip of his coffee, Steve replied, "Well, that's good news. If his perspective about people has changed, that should stop some of the complaints coming in here, shouldn't it?"

"I need to caution you, though." Bill paused. "I know you don't want to hear this, but it will take more than one day of coaching to change the way he interacts with people. But I do think we're moving in the right direction. I'll find out more in a few minutes when I meet with him again, but I'm hopeful that he took some of my advice. Let me ask you: did you get any new complaints about him yesterday?"

Steve brightened up. "Hey, that's right! I checked my voicemail and email, and there were no new Sysol complaints. It's a miracle!" he joked.

"Come on, Steve, give Randy a break. We were both young once, and I can remember some of the mistakes I made when I first started as a leader. I'm sure you had issues as well." Steve nodded his head in agreement. "Not hearing any complaints doesn't mean the problem is fixed, but it may mean we're moving in the right direction. There's a lot more work ahead, but this is a good first step."

"I know. I know, Bill, just let me enjoy it for a minute. I'm glad Randy understands his behavior has been unacceptable. I wasn't sure if his ego would allow even that much. Keep moving the ball forward. We just need to get this behind us so we can focus on the business again. I know you're busy, so I'll let you get back to work."

Bill stood up to leave, then paused by the door. "Steve, one last thing before I go. I want to make sure we're both on the same page: when we talked the other day, we agreed on a weekly update, not on a daily update. You know I don't have the time to meet with you every day to talk about Randy's progress. Can we agree on weekly updates unless something major occurs?"

Steve leaned back in his chair and chuckled. "I can agree to that. Anything else I can do to help?

Bill thought for a moment and then answered, "Yes, there is one more thing. If you see Randy on the floor, don't just focus on his productivity numbers; also ask him how his team is doing. If he thinks the only thing you care about is numbers, it makes my job more difficult. People lead they way they are being led."

"I see your point, Bill. I probably won't see him this week, but if I do, I'll keep your request in mind. So, if that's it, I'll see you on Friday. I need to jump on a conference call with Karnes."

"That's it, boss. See you Friday."

Bill walked briskly back to his office, realizing the meeting had lasted longer than he'd expected. He was trying not to be too hard on Steve's need for information because he understood the pressure on him. He turned the corner toward his office, and was surprised to see Randy sitting in a chair beside the door, going through his notebook.

"Did we get our signals crossed? I wasn't expecting you for another hour."

Randy closed the notebook and smiled. "No, you're right, you said nine, but I couldn't wait to talk to you again. Things went better yesterday!"

Bill couldn't hide his excitement from Randy. "Really? Now that makes me happy! Let me grab a cup of coffee and I'll be right in. Can't wait to hear what went well yesterday."

Bill could have jumped and touched the moon, but he also knew Randy had a huge mountain to climb. Pouring his coffee, he reminded himself that he had to balance Randy's initial success with the reality that he still had a long way to go. He hustled back to his office, spilling a few drops of coffee on his hand as he entered the room.

Bill motioned to Randy to come into his office. "Please have a seat. I see you still have your notebook."

Randy looked at it and held it up. "Yeah. I realize if I want to really learn and develop in our time together, I need to take some notes. There's no way I can remember all this."

Bill laughed out loud and said, "Good, I think you're right. So, things went better for you yesterday, and that's great to hear. Tell me what specifically went well, young man?"

"Remember how yesterday I told you how I'd changed the cycle counting process?"

Bill nodded. "Sure do. You said it was to improve our accuracy and productivity, but the change made a few of your people mad."

"You know Pam and Molly?"

Bill nodded.

Randy continued, "They've been here forever. When I made the change, my goal was to make it easier for them to do their jobs. I wasn't trying to be mean to them. I saw an opportunity to improve a process, so I changed it. I really thought I would get a 'thank you' from both of them."

Bill was puzzled. "Doesn't sound bad to me. Why would Molly and Pam be upset about you making their job easier? They should be thanking you, not criticizing you! What's wrong with them?"

Randy looked confused. "What's wrong with them? Are you serious?"

Bill set his coffee on the desk and continued, "Yeah. Your job is to improve the way we do business here. You saw an inefficiency, so you fixed it. By improving the process, you made their job easier. Why should they be upset with you? You did exactly what we're paying you to do; they should be thanking you."

Randy wondered, *Am I not saying this right?* "Bill, you're missing the point here." Randy took a deep breath to gather his thoughts. "I changed the process without getting their input. They've worked in cycle counting for twenty five years. Twenty five years of dedicated service to the company, then a kid out of college turns things upside down without discussing the situation with them. Like you said yesterday, people want to be valued, but my behavior didn't suggest I valued them. Instead, it insulted them. If it had been me, I'd have been furious. And another thing: if I would have involved them in the decision and gotten their input, I would have realized why the current process was in place and that my changes wouldn't help anything – they actually hurt the business. I didn't have a complete picture of how the system worked. Now do you see why they were upset?"

As Randy finished, Bill reached for his coffee cup, smiling from ear to ear. "I know exactly why they were upset. Everyone wants to be valued and empowered. So you decided to tap into their expertise. Inclusion in decision-making increases commitment to the solution."

Bill stopped for a moment and then asked Randy to write down an important truth: "Most people don't hate change; however, people do hate *being* changed." Bill let Randy write for a moment. "I knew about the situation with Molly and Pam prior to our meeting yesterday. I could have easily told you what to do, but I wanted you to reach that conclusion on your own."

Randy sighed and gave a half-hearted grin. "Well, thanks a lot, friend."

Bill laughed. "No problem! That's what friends are for."

Randy said, "Well, I should tell you, I did ask some more questions about you and your leadership style, with people on the leadership team and with some folks on the floor."

Bill asked, "And what did you find out about me, Randy?"

"Everyone told me you were a 'people guru,' and I'm starting to believe them. You were making me frustrated when you didn't understand the way Pam and Molly felt. I thought either you must have forgotten everything we talked about yesterday or I wasn't making myself clear. I can't believe I fell for it. Try not to take me for such a long walk next time!"

"I can't promise you anything, but I wanted to make sure you understood the concepts we discussed yesterday. How are Molly and Pam now?"

Randy hesitated. "Better. I apologized to them for not getting their input right at the beginning of our conversation. I told them why I did what I did, but I also told them I wanted their input. We sat down in the conference room and they gave me a good education on the system and process. We left on the same page. They thanked me for allowing them to explain the system, and to be part of the decision."

Bill was encouraged to hear that Randy wasn't letting pride be a road block to their goal. "Randy, I'm truly happy for you. That's a good first step in getting aligned with Molly and Pam. How did it go with the rest of the team?"

Randy hesitated, and then said, with a little frustration, "Okay, I guess. I tried reaching out to several of them, with limited success. I started getting frustrated with the lack of progress, but I realized it would take longer than a five-minute chat. I'm not giving up. The main thing is that I'm more confident today than I was yesterday. I saw them as people just like me. Just doing that has changed my perspective and thought process. It will take me some time with several of them. I wish I could do the same thing I did with Molly and Pam with the others. I knew what Pam and Molly needed, and I met their needs."

"It takes time. Some people require more time than others. I'm very proud of you, though. Speaking of needs, did you watch *The Wizard of Oz* last night?"

Randy pulled the DVD out of a front pocket of his folder and handed it over. "Bill, with all due respect, how can *The Wizard of Oz* be your favorite movie of all time? The scenery is fake, the special effects are archaic, the music's not exciting, and the plot's pretty lame. You need to let me pick out the next movie."

Bill laughed. "You're so wrong. That picture has withstood the test of time. It's like Lincoln's quote we discussed yesterday. It's as good today as it was fifty years ago. Enough with your movie critique; did you learn anything from the movie?"

Randy started shaking his head. "Oh yeah. Never go to Kansas during tornado season."

Both men laughed as Bill stood up and went to the whiteboard in his office. He made two columns on the board. One column was labeled "character" and the other was labeled "needs".

CHARACTER	NEEDS

"Let me outline the plot for you. Each of the characters need something different from the wizard. Dorothy wants to go home, the scarecrow wants a brain, the tin man wants a heart, and the lion wants courage." As Bill summarized the movie, he completed the chart on his white board. "Is that correct?"

CHARACTER	NEEDS
Dorothy	To go home
Scarecrow	A brain
Tin Man	A heart
Lion	Courage

Randy smiled and answered, "Yep, that part of the movie I got. The plot wasn't all that deep."

Bill could see that Randy was only focused on his personal viewpoint and said, "Sometimes the simple aspects of life are the richest." Pointing at the board he went on, "So, each character has a specific need. Let's look at Dorothy." Bill circled her name on the board. "The only thing Dorothy wants is to go home. She doesn't want or need anything else. If the Wizard of Oz would have given Dorothy a heart, a brain, or courage, would she be happy?"

Randy quickly answered, "No."

"Why not? The scarecrow would be thrilled with a brain, the tin man ecstatic with a heart, and the lion excited about receiving courage. Why wouldn't she be happy with any of them?"

Randy knew Bill was setting up something, and he wanted to get it right. He said carefully, "Because she doesn't need any of them. She already has them. All she wants is to go home. The rest of the stuff doesn't matter to her. Right?" he asked.

"Absolutely. Dorothy's needs were different than the other characters'. Just like your team. Every person on your team has different needs. The key to motivating your team members is to find out what their individual needs are and give them the opportunity to fulfill those needs. Most managers try to motivate people from the outside in. They use motivators that work for them. But you can't motivate from the outside in; you motivate from the inside out. Motivation is internal. What are the needs of the people on your team, rather than your needs? Let's take a look."

Bill made two more columns on the board. One column was labeled, "Randy's team," which Bill populated with a few of Randy's team members; the other column was labeled "Randy's team's needs."

Randy's team members   **Randy's team's needs**
Brian
Subash
Molly

"Okay, Randy, what are the needs of the individual members of your team? For example, what are Brian Fellinger's needs?" While Randy was thinking about this, Bill took a sip of his coffee. It had grown cold; he set it down and went back to the board.

Randy answered, "I don't know. To be honest, I haven't spent much time with him. He isn't the best example to use for this exercise."

In a stern voice, Bill asked, "Why not? He's a member of your team, isn't he? Are his needs important to you or not?"

"I'm just not sure about Brian." Randy began shaking his head slightly. "The thing with Brian, you know him. He's a disgruntled employee, always has a negative attitude, nothing pleases him. He was like that when I arrived. You can't blame me for his behavior. I inherited this problem. Besides, the way things are going, he may not be around here too much longer. I'm not going to waste my time on a lost cause."

Bill's tone became serious as he explained, "A lost cause? Randy, write this down and remember this: *No one is a lost cause! They may be misdirected, they may lack motivation, they may be unhappy, but everyone can be turned around. We should never give up on people.* Let me ask you a few questions before you write Brian off completely. Why do you think Brian is disgruntled? Do you think it's his fault?"

Randy leaned forward and almost snapped, "It sure isn't my fault!" Randy paused to gain his composure before he continued, "I really don't know why the man is so unhappy with his job. He's probably one of those people who generally hates life and blames everyone for his problems. That's just the way he is, I guess. I am sure you've seen people like him in your career."

Bill stepped back from the board for a moment, rubbing his chin. "Let me ask you another question. When an employee is disgruntled at work, who's to blame for their behavior?"

Randy thought for a moment. "People choose their attitude. I can't control their attitude or behavior; they're responsible for it. I can only control mine. Brian needs to change his behavior – I can't do it for him. If someone did him wrong in the past, he needs to get over it. I can't do anything about that, and anyway, it's not my problem. It's his!"

Bill saw the opening he was looking for. "I agree: you can't control the behavior of other people. But you can have an influence on them. Don't you influence the people on your team?"

Randy responded with little conviction. "I guess so, provided the person is willing to be influenced by me, but they have to be open-minded and willing to listen."

Bill leaned forward in his chair and said, "Randy, leadership is all about influence. Every time we interact with another person, we have an influence, positive or negative. This is a critical point that most leaders don't understand: leaders blow opportunities to positively influence people every day. People's hearts are won in the small moments of life. Those times when you're busy or stressed and you neglect an employee, you influence that person. You communicate to them that their needs are not important."

Randy started writing again. He knew Bill was making a very important point. *How many opportunities have I missed every day to positively influence someone?* he thought.

When Randy stopped writing, Bill asked him, "Randy, how do you think leadership is measured?"

Randy knew he had this one. "Simple. Did the leader make money for the company or not? Did the leader meet their KPI's? It comes down to the bottom line."

Bill left the board and took a few steps toward Randy. "Randy, this point is critical; please write this down. *Leadership is not measured by the bottom line.* The bottom line is a result of your ability to influence. At the end of the month, take a look at your numbers. Your numbers reflect how well you influenced your team that month. The better influence of the leader, the better the numbers. Leadership is measured by the discretionary effort of your team. Are people willing to do things without being asked? The question every leader must ask him or herself is, *Do my people do things because they have to do them, which is the effect of my authority, or do my people do things because they want to do them?* There's a huge difference between authority and influence, and most managers confuse them. It's critical to understand the difference. Managers use authority; leaders use influence. People do not want to be managed, people want to be led. Lead people and manage things. Bad managers make money in the short term. Leaders make money for the long term. They get people to buy into the team concept, and inspire them to do more than they think possible. Many companies lose money because they measure leadership by the bottom line. Yes, the manager made money for the month or year, but they left money on the table. They could have been more profitable if they had a leader using influence rather than a manager using authority. Do you see the importance of leadership influence?"

Randy looked a little overwhelmed by Bill's comments. "To be honest with you, Bill, I've always seen influence and authority as one and the same. My dad had authority and boy, did that influence me to work hard." Both Randy and Bill laughed. "I've never made a distinction between them, but I am starting to see the difference – we can't directly control an employee's behavior, but we play a huge part in shaping it. I just wish I knew how to do it."

Bill closed his eyes as he thought about the best way to explain the concept. "Let me see if I can clarify the difference, and show you how your daily behavior shapes the behaviors of your team. And – you'll like this part, Randy – how your daily behavior impacts your KPI's and the bottom line." Bill grabbed a marker and wrote three more columns on the white board. He titled the first column "needs," the second column "feelings," and the third column "behaviors."

Needs   **Feelings**   **Behaviors**

"Now Randy, what do employees need from their managers? Let me put it another way: if I'm your manager, what do you need from me?"

Randy put his hand to his chin as he began to speak. "Hmmm. I would need you to support me, listen to me, coach me, develop me, value my opinion, keep me updated on the business, and provide feedback to me on my performance. Those are several things I'd like my manager to do for me. I'm sure there are more, but I think I hit the major ones."

Bill listed Randy's comments under the column titled needs.

Needs	Feelings	Behaviors
Support me		
Listen to me		
Coach me		
Provide feedback		
Develop me		
Value my opinion		

Bill reviewed the list and said, "Yeah, I'm sure there are more but I think you got the major ones. Is there anything here that seems like an unreasonable need for an employee to have?"

Randy reviewed the list, "No, I think those are all reasonable expectations that most people have of their manager."

Bill pointed to the first column and said, "I agree. Let me ask you this: if I met all your needs, how would you feel?"

Randy studied the list on the board before answering Bill's question. After a few minutes, he responded, "I would feel important, significant, valued, appreciated, happy, and knowledgeable of what's going on. I can't think of anything else right now but overall, it'd all be good."

"Good." Bill recorded Randy's responses under column two.

Needs	Feelings	Behaviors
Support me	Important	
Listen to me	Significant	
Coach me	Valued	
Provide feedback	Appreciated	
Develop me	Knowledgeable	

Bill pointed to the second column. "One last question, Randy: if you felt that way, how would you behave at work? Take a minute to think about it."

Randy again studied the list Bill had written on the board. "I would be motivated and engaged, my productivity would be good, and I'd be willing to go the extra mile, and with a positive attitude. I would want to come to work, and overall, I'd be a happy employee."

Again, Bill wrote Randy's answers on the white board.

Needs	**Feelings**	**Behaviors**
Support me	Important	More productive
Listen to me	Significant	Positive attitude
Coach me	Valued	Motivated
Provide feedback	Appreciated	Go the extra mile
Develop me	Knowledgeable	Reliable

Just then, Bill's phone rang. He took a step toward his desk without saying anything. He could see it was Steve calling, but not wanting to break the momentum in the room, he gestured to Randy to ignore it, and let it roll to voicemail.

As he walked back to the board he went on, "All employees have certain expectations or needs they need met by their managers. If their manager meets those needs, employees will have these feelings." Bill pointed to the second column. "If employees feel the way you describe here, they will behave in a positive manner. When a person's needs are met, they have positive feelings, and when people have positive feelings, they will have productive and positive behaviors. So can you see how your behavior as a leader can influence the behavior of your employees in a positive direction?"

Randy frowned. "People expect to have certain needs met by their managers, and when their manager meets those needs, they feel good and produce good results. I never really thought about that, Bill."

Bill sat back down at his desk and looked down at his journal. "One quick thing before we move on to my next point. Many times we ask our managers how they're doing as a leader. In reality, it's not that important how your manager thinks you're doing as a leader;

what's important is how the people that work for you think you're doing as a leader."

Randy looked down at the floor and thought for several seconds before he responded to Bill. "It's a great point, but I keep getting this feeling you already know the end of the story of where we're going with my development plan, and you're just methodically walking me through it."

Bill shook his head. "Not true. We're working the plan together, and we'll adapt the plan to your needs and change direction when appropriate. Let's go back to the white board. We know people have needs which determine feelings and results in behavior. Now let's see what happens when employee needs are not met by their manager. You've identified what you needed from me. How would you feel if I didn't meet your needs?" Bill erased what he had written under the second and third columns.

Randy considered and then replied, "Almost the exact opposite: unimportant, betrayed, not valued, angry, and generally unhappy with you."

As Randy spoke, Bill wrote his responses on the board.

Needs	**Feelings**	**Behaviors**
Support me	Unimportant	
Listen to me	Betrayed	
Coach me	Not valued	
Provide feedback	Angry	
Develop me	Unhappy	

Bill pressed on. "Okay, Randy, if you felt that way, how would you behave at work?"

Randy studied the board and answered, "Well, I wouldn't even want to come to work, for one thing. I'd be disengaged with the business; I'd have a negative attitude, my work performance would probably be low, I'd be disgruntled, and would eventually probably leave the organization."

Again, Bill recorded Randy's responses on the board.

Needs	Feelings	Behaviors
Support me	Unimportant	Disengaged
Listen to me	Betrayed	Negative attitude
Coach me	Not valued	Not Productive
Provide feedback	Angry	Disgruntled
Develop me	Unhappy	Leave

"You'd be disgruntled. Why?" smiled Bill.

"Because you didn't meet my needs," answered Randy.

"Exactly. Because," Bill paused for emphasis, "I didn't meet your needs. So the leader caused the person to be disgruntled." Bill paused again to let Randy absorb the concept. "If I meet your needs, you'll be happy; if I don't meet your needs, you'll be disgruntled. Who's the problem here? The employee or the manager? Most of the time when we have a disgruntled employee, we immediately blame the employee, not ourselves. When you have a disgruntled employee, you should first look internally and ask yourself, am I meeting their needs? If you're not meeting their needs, could you be causing their behavior? Most employees want to be successful at work, but they have certain needs. When the leader meets those needs, you can see the positive results, and when their needs are not met, the results are quite different. Make sense to you?"

Randy started writing in his notebook. "There you go again with another great learning point. You're opening me up to a whole new way of thinking." Randy paused, "When I see a disgruntled employee, I blame the person. Now that I see it on the board, though, I realize there's more to it." He paused again. "I never looked at it like you outlined on the board before. I can see how my behavior influences others and directly impacts a person's behavior. Your chart is really eye-opening. It's easy to blame the person, isn't it?"

Bill shook his head. "It is very easy, and most managers blame the person without examining their own behavior first. Most managers don't believe it could be their fault the person is disgruntled. Let's go back to Brian Fellinger. Is it possible Brian is disgruntled because his needs as an employee have not been met by his manager? I understand that you have only been his supervisor for two months. But is it possible that in the past, Brian's needs were not met by his manager, and that's why he behaves the way he does?"

Randy answered immediately, "Based on our discussion today, it seems like a strong possibility. I haven't helped the situation either, because I've basically left him alone. To be honest, I wrote the man off. I don't have any idea what makes the man tick, his background, work history, or anything." Randy seemed bothered by this admission and put his head in his hand.

Bill returned to his desk. "You have some work to do with Brian this week. You need to get to know him. I hired Brian, and I can tell you that he wasn't disgruntled when we hired him. Find out why he isn't happy here anymore. I think you'll be surprised."

"I get the feeling you already know the answer to your question, and I also know you're not going to tell me if I ask. I suppose I need to find the answer myself. What are you, Yoda?" Randy grinned.

Bill laughed at Randy's comment as he picked up his journal. "No, I'm not Yoda, but am I really that predictable?"

Randy said enthusiastically, "Yes, you are that predictable. What's next?"

Bill reviewed his notes again. "I just want to make one last point on influence before we move to another topic. In order for a person to influence you, do you have to trust the person?"

Randy responded quickly, "If I don't trust a person, I don't even want to be around him or her. Trust in my world is an absolute requirement for me in any relationship."

Bill picked up Randy's resume and remarked, "I know you've only been here for a few months, but let's look at your internship at Petersen Distribution Solutions. You were responsible for leading fifteen associates for twelve weeks. Is that correct?"

Randy responded quickly, "It was more like twenty or twenty-five when you include the temporary employees."

Bill picked up his pen and made a note on Randy's resume before he asked his next question. "Okay, twenty or twenty-five employees you led for twelve weeks. Out of those twenty-five people, did you have a high level of influence over some of them?"

Randy thought for a moment. "In my mind, yes. I'm not sure I can give you the exact number, but it was more than half of them."

Bill took a sip of coffee and asked his next question. "Would the rest of your team at Petersen fall into a category of moderate influence over some of them and low influence over others?"

Randy paused again; he knew he had an influence on them, but to what degree? "I would say most of them were in the moderate category, with just a few people in the low influence category."

"Fair enough, Randy; let's focus on the people you put in the low influence category. You told me that in order for a person to influence you, you had to trust the person. Given you had little influence over these people, why didn't they trust you?"

Randy grinned and sat back in his chair. "Bill, you don't play fair. You ask me questions to set me up. That is wrong, so wrong, though I have to give you credit: you're a masterful interrogator. You're always one step ahead of me."

Bill tilted his head toward Randy. "Trust me, I'm not trying to set you up at all. Remember, we're partners in your development plan. I'm trying to facilitate a process that allows you to explore other leadership options. We all need to have our beliefs challenged from time to time. When you have a low level of influence over people, in most cases it comes down to trust. In such cases, there are two questions you need to ask yourself: what do I need to do to establish trust with them? Or, what have I done to break the trust with the person?" Bill paused, because Randy had started writing again; he did not him want to forget this point, and he could see things were coming together. Bill asked next, "So, with the team you led at Petersen, which was it for you?"

"I didn't establish trust with some of them. It was all about getting freight out of the building and I never connected with a few of them. If you don't have trust, you can't influence them." Randy rubbed his eyes with his hand. "Bill, as you can tell, I have a lot to learn about leading people."

Bill smiled and responded, "Randy, so do I. Heck, all leaders have a lot to learn about leadership. Remember, it's a journey, not a destination." Randy nodded his head in agreement. "Going back to *The Wizard of Oz*, each of your employees have needs, and most of them have different needs. If you're not meeting their needs, they're not buying into you. If they don't buy into you, they will never buy into your vision. For the next two days, I want you to spend time with each employee, finding out what is important to them. What are their needs? What are their goals? What are their dreams? What are their expectations of you? When we get together next, we can cover your progress. Sound like a plan?"

"Bill, my head is swimming right now. I have pages of notes, and I'm trying to process it all. Leading people is more than just knowing how to get a product in and out of the building. I never really put much emphasis on the people part. I do have a question about that, actually. What is the balance between people and business? I see why the people side is important, but it still seems like too much focus on the people side could hurt you on the business side. Am I making any sense?"

Bill could see that although Randy's mind was opening up to new ideas, he was still trying to protect its "all about the numbers" mentality. "Randy, yes, you are making sense; follow me for a minute. Remember our discussion yesterday? A leader's orientation toward people and toward productivity isn't an either-or proposition. One is not done to the exclusion of the other. Good leaders have the ability to meet the needs of the business and at the same time meet the needs of their people. Globalistics has to make a profit; there's nothing wrong with making money. If you don't hold people accountable, you won't make money, and this conversation would be totally different. I'm not suggesting the business aspect isn't important, and I'm not suggesting that we don't need to hold people accountable, but we as leaders have a huge impact on the bottom line and on our team's behavior just by the way we lead. Like I said earlier, bad managers still make money."

Randy nodded. "I remember you saying that earlier, but how can a bad manager still make money? The statement doesn't make any sense to me."

"Good question. Let me give you an example. We had a general manager a few years back at our Fredonia facility who made the business roughly a million dollars annually. I would classify him as a task master: no nonsense, bottom line-oriented type of guy. He was a manager, not a leader. I visited his facility several times, and was always impressed by the site's cleanliness and the professionalism of the staff, but I always left feeling like people were not truly happy working there. You never saw anyone smiling or looking cheerful. I knew if that site had had a leader running it, we'd make more money than we currently were. We were underperforming, and eventually we did replace him with a leader; the next year we made five million dollars at the site. The first guy wasn't a good leader, but on the financial reports, he made money. He was a bad manager, and he still made money. Most financial people would argue the first guy made us one million dollars, but in my view, he lost the company four million dollars. We were measuring his performance wrong. We only measured the financials, not the impact his behavior was having on the facility. Like I said earlier, leadership is not measured by the bottom line, it's measured by the discretionary effort of your followers. Once we replaced him, the work culture there changed, and we ended up making more money with a real leader. Sorry for getting up on my soap box, but I believe this stuff from the top of my head to the tips of my toes."

Randy grinned and leaned forward in his chair. "There's no doubt in my mind, Bill: you believe the stuff we're discussing. You won't get any argument from me. I really do need to internalize this idea that leading people is more than meeting numbers, and it's about people and relationships with them. I hate to admit this, but that interpersonal communication class isn't looking so silly right now, and I'm not looking forward to the debate you promised me yesterday – I think I already lost. Should I come by tomorrow at the same time?"

Bill was laughing as he responded. "I thought you may reconsider your comments about the class. I won't be able to meet with you for the rest of the week, but will be available by phone if you have any questions. I was hoping we could hook up on Saturday. I found this nice fishing hole down the street from my house and was wondering if you'd like to join me Saturday for a little fishing."

Randy's eyes lit up. "I'd love to. I'm not much of a fisherman – well I know how, but I do need a little relaxation. Since I moved here it has been all work and no play. It will be great to get away from the facility for a day and breathe some fresh air. What time and where should I meet you?"

"I'll send you an email with all the information. I do have a few more minutes; any other questions?"

"Let me think . . ." Randy looked back through his notes, "Oh, yeah. You mentioned several times today that leadership isn't measured by the bottom line, it's measured by the 'discretionary effort' of a leader's team. Can you give me an example of what you mean by discretionary effort?"

"Hmmm. Yes, I have a perfect one for you, from just the other day. I was flying to Dallas for a seminar and I forgot my cell phone in the airport bathroom. I quickly ran back to the bathroom, but it was gone. I asked one of the security guards if anyone turned in a cell phone, but no one had. I didn't have time to go to the lost and found. I hate being without my cell phone; I almost feel naked without it."

Randy laughed. "I know exactly what you mean. It's part of my wardrobe."

"I kind of hate that too, but it is part of our way of life. But back to my story. When I arrived in Dallas, I called Mary Spain and asked her to send an email to the HR community and Steve, to let him know I had lost my phone, so they would have to call the hotel or communicate to me by email. I checked into the hotel room and thirty minutes later I received a phone call from Mike Wallace. You know Mike, he's one of the HR representatives here. He reports to me."

"Yeah, I know Mike. He did my orientation. He's a really nice guy. I heard he was a great quarterback."

"He was a great quarterback; I played midget league football with him. He's an integral part of my team now......" Bill had lost his train of thought. "Where was I?"

"You were telling me Mike called the facility you were at."

"Yes, he called the facility, and he told me that after reading the email, he had called the airport's lost and found department, and they had my cell phone. The people at the airport told him I could pick up my phone when I returned, but he knew I needed my phone sooner, so he arranged to have the phone shipped overnight so that it would arrive in Dallas by ten the next morning. I didn't ask him to do it; he just took it upon himself. He told me I would have done the same thing for him. That's discretionary effort: people doing things because they want to, not because they have to. Does that answer your question?"

Randy wrote Bill's last statement down. "I think I understand now. Thanks."

Bill stood up and shook Randy's hand "I'll send you an email with the directions and time of our meeting this weekend." Bill's phone began to ring. "I need to take this call. See you Saturday."

Randy smiled and left Bill's office as Bill answered the phone and began talking about his hiring plan with Jack O'Connor.

Chapter Six
Fishing Lures

Saturday morning, Bill was returning home from the bait shop where he had picked up some night crawlers and minnows for the fishing excursion with Randy. He couldn't help feeling like a little kid again. He could remember the times when the "Washington Avenue Gang" would go on their annual fishing trips during college. They didn't catch many fish, but they always had a great time. As he was getting his fishing poles and tackle box together, his cell phone rang. He could see from the caller ID that it was Steve. He had to hope Steve had read his email explaining Randy's progress, because he didn't have much time to spend on the phone with him. He had to finish packing the fishing gear, and he knew Randy would soon be there.

"Good morning, Steve," he answered. "I missed you yesterday. I came by your office but Mary said you were in a meeting with Tom Karnes and didn't think I should disturb you. Did you get my email recapping my second meeting with Randy? As you can see, I think we're making real progress with him."

Steve replied enthusiastically, "Looks like the magic man is working his magic. I was ecstatic with your update, my friend. It was extremely encouraging news. I think you were right, Randy does seem to have the right attitude to make the changes required. He just needed some coaching and development."

"I'm not sure about any magic, but I agree the initial results are encouraging. We still have a ways to go. Any other questions, boss?"

"Don't be so modest, Bill. You know you're good at this stuff. Anyway, on another note, I ran into Molly yesterday out in the parking lot and asked how things were going. She told me about the meeting she and Pam had with Randy. She had some very positive things to say about him. She had some concerns at first, but their conversation went a long way towards mending fences with her. It has been a week and a half, and not one complaint from the floor. It's wonderful to have a positive report for Karnes. Perhaps he'll start focusing back on the business, instead of just the Sysol situation. One last thing before I let you go: your email mentioned a fishing excursion with Randy today. What's this all about?"

"It's all part of the plan. Ouch, I just snagged myself with a lure, give me one minute." Bill removed the lure from his shirt sleeve and put it in the tackle box. "Randy mentioned he'd like some fishing tips, so I thought we could spend the morning fishing. Get him out of the facility in an informal situation. Give him a chance to relax a little bit, and me a chance to get caught up with him on his week. Besides, it's a great excuse to get out of some yard work." Bill looked out the window. "He just pulled up to the house. I need to get out there. Anything else you need?"

"No, have a great day. Keep the ball rolling."

"Will do Steve, talk to you next week." Bill hung up the phone and went out to the front yard to greet Randy.

Bill waved to Randy to pull his truck into the driveway. Randy parked and grabbed his poles and tackle boxes from the bed of his Ford Ranger. Bill was amazed at the size of his tackle box; he had never seen one that big before. *For someone that doesn't fish much, that's massive. I wonder what he brings when he goes hunting.*

Jokingly, Bill said, "Hey, we're not going deep sea fishing for marlin, it's just a small fishing pond on my friend's farm. That thing may scare the fish away."

Randy laughed. "When I'm committed to something, I don't go halfway. I take my fishing seriously. Ah, not really, but I wanted to look the part. I may not catch a fish, but I'll look good doing it." They both laughed as Randy continued, "These aren't mine; I borrowed them from Henry Hooton. I told Henry this tackle box was overkill, but he assured me I'd need everything in it."

Bill smiled. "I'm sure it does have everything you need. I should have told you I had an extra pole for you, and I also went out and got some bait for us. Throw your stuff in the back of my truck and we'll be on our way. Just need to go tell my wife we're leaving."

Randy put his poles and boxes in the back of Bill's truck while Bill stepped back inside. He called up the stairs, "Hey babe, Randy's here and we're heading out."

"Hold on a minute. Am I ever going to meet this young man you're spending so much time with?" Casey called back.

Bill answered, "Of course you will, but we need to get to the pond before the wind picks up. The conditions are perfect right now. Maybe next week we can all meet for lunch."

His wife came down the stairs; she smiled at Bill and said, "Get going, then. I don't want to be your excuse if you don't catch anything. Be careful, and remember you're not a kid anymore."

"I will, babe." As Bill briskly walked out the door he added over his shoulder, "I love you, honey!"

Bill hopped into the truck and began driving toward Raynor's Pond. As they drove, they discussed the upcoming game between the Boston Red Sox and the New York Yankees. Bill was a big Sox fan and Randy a big Yankees fan. They teased each other about the outcome of the game and why their favorite team was going to win. Randy couldn't imagine how Bill could have been born and raised in New York State and love the Red Sox. Something about that just didn't seem right.

Bill pointed to a sprawling white farm house on the right hand side of the road. "There it is. This is a beautiful place. Nick Sobecki owns over five thousand acres here. He raises cattle, chickens, and soy beans, and for a hobby he trains German Shepherds for the K9 division of the New York State Police. He's one busy guy. Is the smell of the country making you homesick yet?"

Randy was taking in all the sights. "It's bringing back some good memories. I love being out in the country. My dad owns eleven hundred acres and two hundred head of cattle. He grows primarily corn and soy bean and hay, of course. At times I do get a little homesick for the farm, but when I think of those hundred-degree days baling hay, the feeling goes away really quick. How do you know Nick?"

"Nick and I went to high school together. We both played football. I was the quarterback and he played running back. He got a football scholarship to Harvard. He's a super bright person, played four years of college football while maintaining a 4.0 GPA. I still don't know how he did it. I struggled making a 3.3 from Mercyhurst. He graduated from Harvard with a degree in organizational behavior, received his MBA from George Washington University in Washington D.C., went to Wall Street, and became an executive there. Nick is a true success story."

Randy interrupted. "Hold on a minute. A graduate from Harvard, an MBA, Wall Street executive now lives on a farm and raises cows and chickens? What went wrong with his career?"

Bill turned and looked at Randy thoughtfully. "Nothing. Quite the opposite. He made a ton of money, but he always dreamed of living in the country farming. He hated the rat race of New York City. Once he made his money, he quit his firm and moved here. He couldn't be happier with his life. I've learned more about people from him than anyone else."

"That's quite a compliment for Nick, coming from you. It's just hard to believe that he had what most people dream of, and he walked away from it to farm. That's unreal. I would love to meet him someday," Randy said.

Bill was not ignorant of the youthful, ambitious dreams of a young man out to conquer the world. "His story is different, but he's one of the lucky people in life. Everyone needs to find out what their passion is. His passion wasn't Wall Street, it was Main Street America. He's living his dream. How many people go to a job they hate each day? Think about Globalistics and the people there." Bill could see Randy was processing the discussion in his mind. "When we get done fishing, let's see if Nick is around and I'll introduce you to him. But first things first; we have some fish to catch." Bill pulled his truck up to the pond. "Grab the poles; it's time to separate the men from the boys."

The two men gathered up their fishing equipment, two chairs, and a cooler of sodas, and headed to the pond. It was hard to tell who was more excited.

"Randy, this is what life is all about. Sitting back, relaxing, and enjoying the fresh air with good company. It's like the MasterCard commercials: 'Priceless.'" Both men laughed loudly. "I'm really glad you could come fishing with me today. Hopefully the fish will cooperate and let us catch them. What do you think?"

Randy nodded in full agreement. "*Priceless* is correct. I appreciate the invite. I've been so focused on my job, I needed a break from the grind. I really haven't done anything but work since I moved to Dunkirk, so you won't hear any complaints from me."

The two men began casting their lines into the water. Bill began fishing with minnows and Randy was using worms. After about thirty minutes without any nibbles, Bill decided to change to worms as well. Despite the lack of success, they were enjoying each other's company and sharing their views on various topics. Bill made a deliberate point of not discussing anything work-related. He was starting to realize that Randy had similar values to his despite their age difference, and he was really enjoying Randy's company.

After an hour of casual conversation, Randy looked at Bill and said,

"I'm surprised that you haven't asked me about work yet, and how I did with my team. Not interested?"

Bill grabbed a Coke from the cooler and answered, without looking directly at Randy, "No, I'm very interested on how you did these last few days, but I thought we could spend some time getting to know each other better. We've been so focused on work, we haven't had much of a chance to discuss anything else. But now that we've solved the world's problems, how did you do with your assignment?"

Randy reeled in his bait, brought his rod back, and cast his line near some cattails. "Well . . . overall, it went pretty well. I got mixed results, but there were some positive things that came out of the last few days. Even spent some time with . . . "

Before Randy could finish his thought, Bill interrupted, "Hold that thought because I got myself a fish! Sit back and take notes, grasshopper, and let the master show you how it's done."

The expression on Bill's face was priceless. Randy would have thought he had hooked Orca when the fish first hit his line. He began to reel his catch to shore, but his bravado at getting the first fish diminished slightly when he pulled up his catch. He had caught a six-inch carp.

"I knew it wasn't a huge fish by the tug on the line, but I was expecting something a little bigger. I was sure it was at least a bass. I didn't really want a carp."

Randy tried to hide his smile and not laugh at Bill's catch. He had thought by Bill's reaction that he had a huge one. "Well, Master, it's not a big fish, but at least you caught something. I haven't even got a nibble yet. Look on the bright side: if we run out of bait, we can use your fish."

Bill tried to conceal his disappointment. "Funny, Randy, very funny; don't quit your day job just yet. But remember, regardless of the size, I did catch the first fish."

"You did catch the first fish, and I'd have rubbed it in as well if I had gotten the first one. But I'm confident that we'll catch some bigger fish today," replied Randy.

"I agree; we'll get bigger ones. I really want to pull out a few crappie or bass today. Oh well, can't catch anything with my line out of the water. Please continue with your update."

As Randy began to speak, Bill changed his bait again. This time he put on medium-sized spinner bait. It was one of those colorful ones with the fluffy mid-section. "I lost my train of thought," Randy mused, "give me a minute. Oh yeah, I had a chance to spend some time with Brian on Thursday."

"Good, how did that go?" asked Bill.

Randy tugged on his line a little, hoping the worm would move and draw some attention of any fish passing by. "Not bad. I tried to get to know him better, as you suggested. He seems like a nice guy. He was much different than I thought. He didn't go into a lot of detail about his last supervisor, but he gave me enough background to understand why he's not the happiest camper in the building. Apparently two years ago he signed up on a posting for an inventory control position and had an interview. He didn't get the position. He's not upset about not getting the position, but he is upset about the way he was treated after the process by his supervisor."

Bill shook his head in agreement and said, "I remember that situation. Four people applied for the position and the position was given to John Reed. John's background and experience with a previous company made him a better candidate for the job. Over the next two months, Brian's attitude went down the drain. I always thought it was because he wasn't chosen for the position."

As Bill completed his thought, he felt another strike on his line. "Now this one's a fighter." Randy could tell by the look on Bill's face that he was enjoying the struggle of bringing in the fish. "This is more like it! It has to be at least ten inches." As he netted the fish he crowed,

"Looks more like twelve! It's a crappie, too. Good eating fish, but this is a catch and-release pond. Well partner, looks like it's Bill, two; Randy, zero. You might want to change your bait. The fish aren't hitting on your worm. You want to try one of these spinners? I have a variety, in all colors."

Randy reeled his bait in and cast it out further this time. He was certain all the commotion had scared his fish away. "I'll stick with my worm, thank you." Randy's frustration at being shut out was beginning to show. "I believe in planning your work and working your plan. My plan was to use a night crawler today. Henry told me it was the best type of bait for this time of the year, and now I need to work my plan. You may catch more fish than me today, but I am going to catch the biggest one."

"Suit yourself, Randy. Getting back to Brian, if he wasn't upset about not getting the job, what was the reason for his negative attitude?"

Randy was enjoying the fact that he knew something about someone on his team and Bill didn't. "Don't get me wrong, he was disappointed that he wasn't successful. He really wanted that job. The reason his attitude and behavior changed was the feedback and lack of respect given to him by his supervisor. I think he said his former supervisor's name was Frankie Jagoda . . . ?" Bill nodded and Randy went on, "Frankie told him the other person had more experience for the position and that was the basis for his decision. Brian accepted his explanation. What upset him was that Frankie then tried to steer Brian toward a maintenance position."

Bill remembered Brian mentioning his past work history. "That's because Brian had worked as a mechanic early in his life at one of our competitors, though he didn't like it," replied Bill.

"Brian told me that, but it wasn't just dislike; he said he hated it. He did it for three years and it was the reason he left The Marauder Group and came here. He told Frankie the entire story, stressing how unhappy he was as a mechanic. He asked Frankie to help him develop his skills for an inventory role so the next time one came up he would have a better chance at it."

"Sounds like a reasonable request. Hold on a minute, I have another bite." Bill he smiled at Randy. "This is another good-sized fish. Is this number three or four? I'm starting to lose count."

"It's number three." While Bill took his catch off the hook, Randy continued the conversation about Brian. "Frankie basically continued to push Brian toward the maintenance department." Randy paused for a moment to see if Bill was grasping what he was telling him. "I couldn't believe it. He told Frankie how miserable he had been as a mechanic, but it was like it wasn't registering with Frankie. He kept on –"

"Randy, I'm sorry, but before you go any further, does Brian's situation remind you of anyone or thing we discussed on Tuesday?"

Randy reflected for a moment, trying to recall their discussion earlier in the week. His eyes opened wide and he replied enthusiastically, "Your analogy of Dorothy from *The Wizard of Oz*. She didn't need or want a brain, a heart, or courage, she wanted to go home. That was her need; those other things didn't matter to her. Brian didn't want a position in maintenance; he wanted a role in inventory. That was his need. Awesome!"

"It is awesome! You're starting to connect the dots. One thing though, you bashed the movie the other day. Changed your mind yet? Have any of your so-called action thriller movies provided you with any guidance in your profession like *The Wizard of Oz* has?"

Randy didn't say a word.

"I'm waiting . . ." Bill said, staring straight ahead.

Randy knew Bill had a good point. "You got me. Maybe the movie was better than I thought. But enough about my ability to critique movies. Because his supervisor failed to meet, heck, even acknowledge, his needs, Brian basically checked out of work. He decided to come in to work, do his eight hours, and leave. His philosophy is, 'why should I care about the business when the business doesn't care about me?'" Randy looked at his pole and shook his head. "It amazes me how fast an engaged employee can become disengaged. Frankie didn't connect with him. It's all about leadership influence, because Brian definitely had the drive. I reviewed his personnel file and performance reviews, and he was rated as an above-average performer on three reviews. The other year he received an 'exceeds' rating. He's a good employee. On his review prior to the interview, Frankie commented on Brian's can-do attitude. His current behavior was caused by his supervisor not meeting his needs. Okay, what are you grinning about now?"

"Two things: one, I have another fish on my line, and two, you got the *Wizard of Oz* concept about people's needs. Let me reel this thing in, and then I want to ask you a question."

Bill reeled in his catch; it was another rather large crappie. This one was about thirteen inches long. "This is a nice fish, but man, I want to catch a bass. Nick said there are some five- to six-pounders in the pond, and I love the fight they put up when you catch them. It's a real challenge to bring them in. I'm going to change lures one more time. Maybe this one right here will attract one of those six-pounders to strike." Bill put on a deep-diving crank bait, one of those three inch jobs that looked like a baby bluegill or crappie. "Please feel free to use any of my lures."

Randy was getting frustrated; at this point he just wanted to catch one big fish. "I'll stick with my worms. I feel a big one coming very soon."

Trying to add a little humor to the moment, Bill held up his hands and said, "Suit yourself, but I think the score is now four to zip."

Randy gave a weak smile. "I can count. What's your question? I need to get my mind off the beating I'm taking from you."

"Sounds like you made a breakthrough with Brian. Have you ever thought about your role as a provider of hope?"

Randy reeled his hook in again, checked to make sure there was even any bait on it, and then cast it near the area where Bill was catching his fish. "I've described my role as many things, but hope-provider is not one of them. Not doubt there's a learning point for me here, so let's hear it."

"Randy, I know these four things about people: People can live for four weeks without food, four days without water, four minutes without oxygen – but people can't live four seconds without hope. When people don't have hope in their lives, they quit. People will continue to work hard as long as they have hope for a better tomorrow. As long as they can see the light at the end of the tunnel, they'll keep moving forward. Our role as a leader is to provide people with the hope of a better tomorrow. Do you think Jagoda provided Brian with the hope of a better tomorrow?"

Without any hesitation Randy responded, "Absolutely not. In fact, instead of providing hope for Brian, he took his hope way."

Bill tightened his line and continued, "You're exactly right. He wasn't a hope provider, he was a dream stealer. What a shame to take a motivated employee and turn him into a disgruntled employee. If leaders could understand how their behavior impacts others, what a different place the world would be. Do you think if your behavior gave Brian hope of a better tomorrow, he might come around?"

Randy looked away to avoid eye contact with Bill and responded, "It won't happen overnight, but it can be done. Brian is really down on Dunkirk and doesn't have much respect or trust for our leadership team right now, but that can be changed, with time and commitment. You may have something with this hope concept."

Bill reeled in his line and said, "When you see Brian on Monday, take your supervisor hat off and put on your hope provider hat and see what happens. I think you'll be surprised at the outcome." Randy nodded in agreement. "Randy, did you suffer any setbacks with anyone on your team this week?"

Randy hesitated for a moment and then spoke. "I wouldn't classify them as setbacks, I would call them hurdles. My approach with most people worked fine. I felt a connection with them. Some went better than others, but for the most part, the door is open and I've got one foot inside the house. There were a few people I didn't feel the connection with like I had with the some of the others. Didn't feel the electricity, if that makes sense to you? I don't understand why, either. I did everything exactly the same. My approach especially didn't work with Rich Catalono and Tom Damon. It's a little puzzling to me."

He looked at Bill for guidance. Bill asked, "Why don't you think it worked with those two? Usually they're pretty friendly guys."

"Last night I gave it some good thought and based on my analysis, it came down to a timing issue."

"A timing issue? What do you mean by that?" asked Bill.

Randy cast his line back into the water before he responded to Bill's question. "I didn't get a chance to talk to either of them until late in the day on Friday. They probably were thinking about the weekend. I know I start shutting down mentally by the end of the week. I chose the wrong time to broach the topic; I should have kept it light. I should have talked about their plans for the weekend instead. First thing Monday morning, when they're fresh, I'll circle back to them. I'm confident it will be different then."

Bill pondered Randy's comment for a moment and said, "I agree that it might have been a timing issue. Timing in life is everything. Some interactions just go better at certain times than others. But what is your contingency plan if you don't make a connection with them on Monday?"

Randy was confused by the question. "A contingency plan for a conversation with two of my employees? I don't have a contingency plan." Randy turned toward Bill and said confidently, "If my approach worked with other people on the team, it will work with them. People are people. M&Ms, right? Like I said, I truly believe it was a problem with timing, not of style."

"All right, but just speaking hypothetically, what if it was a style issue, and not a timing issue? I'm not saying it wasn't just the timing, as it very well could have been, but just suppose for a moment it wasn't. Humor me on this one, Randy. What then?"

Randy hesitated for a moment, not to think about the question, but because he was sure he had just seen his bobber go under the water . . . nope, still sitting there. "I won't give up on them, if that's where you're going with this. I'm committed to seeing this through just like everything else, and if I'm consistent with my behavior, they'll eventually come around. I need to open up the lines of communication."

Bill sat down in his chair. "I know you won't give up on them, but have you considered a different approach?"

Randy stared straight ahead. "I don't think a different approach is needed. I really don't. My approach is just fine, you'll see. It worked great with Molly and Pam. I'll call you Monday after I talk to them. It was definitely a timing issue. I don't want to change something that works. You know the old saying, 'if it isn't broke, don't fix it.'"

Bill could see by Randy's facial expression and body posture that he was becoming defensive about the situation, and Bill was afraid Randy was going to shut down on him. He knew he had to proceed with some caution. Before he could say anything else, his pole dipped towards the water. He had another bite. It couldn't have come at a better time, as it broke the tension between the two of them.

"I can't believe it, but I got another one. I bet it's a bass, from the fight it's putting up." He continued reeling in the fish, enjoying the battle with his catch. He could see it thrashing in the water. "Sure enough, it's a bass!" Bill exclaimed. "Randy, could you please grab the net? I don't want to lose it."

Randy grabbed the net and helped Bill land an eighteen-inch bass that must have weighed three or four pounds. "It's not the ten-pound bass I was looking to catch, but it's still a bass." Still looking at the fish, Bill added, "Randy, sorry if my questioning has frustrated you. That's not my intent. I'm trying to get you to explore other options just in case you still don't make the connection with them. Enough of that, let's analyze our fishing results so far."

Randy's competitive side was beginning to show. "I know where this is going: Bill has five and Randy has zero, right?"

"Yeah, those are the results so far, but actually, I don't want to analyze just the results. Instead, let's analyze the process of getting those results. At the beginning of the day, how were each of us doing?"

Randy, trying to shake his sour mood, said, "Not very good. I don't think you caught your first fish for at least an hour. You know my total for the day. So our collective results have been poor."

"Did I do anything differently after that first hour, when I wasn't getting any bites?"

"Let me think about it." Randy closed his eyes briefly. "You stopped using the minnows and went to worms. You changed the type of bait you were using."

"Correct: I changed what I was using to catch fish. My approach wasn't working. I was using live bait and went to a spinner lure. Did it work?'

"Yep, you caught the carp on the worm. You were happy about catching a fish, if not overly enthusiastic about the type and size of it."

"Did I keep using the worms as bait?" asked Bill.

Randy gestured to Bill's tackle box and answered, "No, I think you changed to that spinner thing."

"Exactly. I didn't want to continue to catch carp; I wanted to catch some crappie or bass. Up to that point, the bait I was using wasn't attracting either one, so I switched to a different lure. How did that impact my results? Did I accomplish one of my goals?"

Randy was starting to see the process Bill was talking about. "Mission accomplished. I think the next three fish you caught were all crappie. But you still wanted the ten-pound bass that Nick told you about, so you changed to another lure."

Bill knew he had Randy's attention now. He didn't waste any more time; he went for the main point of the fishing trip. "By changing to another lure, I caught a bass and accomplished my goals for the day. You, on the other hand, never changed your bait, and did you attract any fish?"

Randy smiled and answered, "Heck, I didn't even get a bite with my worms."

Bill nodded. "That's right. You used the same approach all day even though you weren't getting any results. Do you think the outcome might have been different if you'd changed your bait?"

"I can't say with a hundred percent certainty, but probably. Probably would have caught at least one fish. Don't know for sure if it would have worked, but the approach I was using didn't get the job done, either."

"Do you see the point here, Randy? By changing my approach, I changed the results. Different lures attract different types of fish. Tomorrow I could go fishing again, use the same lures I used to catch the crappie and bass today, and not catch anything. But I know one thing: if those lures weren't working tomorrow, I wouldn't use them all day; I'd try different lures. Like the saying goes, 'the definition of insanity is doing the same thing over and over again and expecting different results.' I'd change my approach. And I use the same methodology with people. You can't lead everyone the same way. If you do, some people will think you're the best thing since sliced bread, but others will be lukewarm towards you, and some wouldn't like to work for you at all. Are you still with me?"

Randy's was beginning to see the larger picture. "I think I know where you're going with this."

Bill smiled, encouraged to see that Randy was truly interested in the important concept that was unfolding. "Good. Just humor me for a few more minutes, and then I'll get off my soapbox." Both of them smiled. "I've seen so many leaders fail to understand this concept. They keep using the same approach with every employee they have on their team, over and over and over again, and they get frustrated when half their team isn't on board with them. But they've never connected with those people. Instead of changing their approach, they blame their employees, label them as malcontents. It's absolutely crazy!"

Bill reached into his tackle box and pulled out two different lures, which he held up for Randy to see. "I just want to stand up on a chair and scream at the top of my lungs, 'They're not hitting on your lure! Change your bait! Your approach isn't working, and won't work!' They don't understand that you connect with each person differently."

Holding one of the lures up in the air, Bill continued, "One approach may work with some people, but not with everyone. When it's not working with some people, change your approach, until you find one that will work for them. Use a different lure! Now let's get back to my hypothetical question. What if the problem with Catalano and Damon wasn't a timing issue, but an approach issue? What are you going to do?"

Now, Randy knew the answer to this question, and could reply with confidence, "I need a contingency plan. If the problem isn't a timing issue, I need to change my approach, or as you would say, change my bait. Use a different lure. So do I keep using a different approach until I connect with them?"

"Good question, Randy! That's the challenge for leaders to work out. What lure will each employee hit on? It's difficult because your approach may work one day with someone, and the next day when a different issue comes up, you use the same approach, and they don't bite. So you need to change your style once again. Is it challenging? Yes. Is it impossible? No. The best tool in your leadership tool kit isn't the computer system, or the performance appraisal form, or our coaching process. The best tool in your leadership tool kit is you. Use all of your ability, don't give up on people, don't get comfortable with just one style, and keep trying different approaches until they hit your bait. Eventually, most people will bite."

Randy was in a much better mood now; he had forgotten about the fish he hadn't caught, and was thinking about the valuable concept he had just learned. He told Bill, "I'm so glad we met today. Otherwise, if things don't work out with Rich and Tom on Monday, I wouldn't have had a contingency plan. I probably would have gotten frustrated and blamed them. It could have been a setback for us. Another great lesson in leadership: *Leaders need to change their bait.*"

Bill put his lures back in his tackle box. "Thanks. Had enough fishing for today?" Randy nodded. "Let's pack up and go see if Nick is around. I would love for you to meet him."

They packed the fishing gear into the truck and drove up to Nick's house. When they arrived, Nick was coming out of the door with a cup of coffee in his hand.

Nick waved and called, "How did the fishing trip go?"

Bill looked at Randy and said, "We had a great time, caught a few fish, but most importantly, we had a chance to get to know one another." He didn't mention any numbers, not wanting to embarrass

Randy in front of Nick about being shut out. Bill introduced Randy to Nick and the three of them engaged in small talk for a few moments. "We were hoping to get a few minutes with you," Bill told Nick. "I wanted you to give Randy an opportunity to glean some of your vast knowledge about leadership and people."

Nick chuckled. "Not sure how much he would glean. I'd love to spend a few minutes with him, but I'm running late for a meeting with the Farm Bureau and need to scoot. Can we get together next Friday? I cook a mean hamburger, and it'll give me a chance to test out my homemade lemonade on both of you. I think I've perfected the recipe."

"I never pass up a free meal," Randy grinned. "Sure thing. How would 11:45 a.m. be?"

"Sounds good to me. 11:45 it is. I'm looking forward to getting caught up with you, Bill. Haven't seen you since you went out to work on that start-up. And Randy, you can pick my brain all you want. Not sure if you'll learn much, but I'll share what I know."

The men shook hands, and Randy and Bill headed back toward Bill's house. "How are you feeling about meeting with Rich and Tom on Monday?" Bill asked.

"I'm a little nervous about it. I need to give it some thought tomorrow and come up with a game plan. One thing's for sure, I'm going to try a new lure with them if I don't connect."

They arrived at Bill's house. Bill helped Randy with his fishing gear and the two men said goodbye. As Randy drove away, Bill reflected on the day, feeling good about where Randy was headed in his development.

Chapter Seven
Rosetta Stone

Bill arrived at the warehouse at 7:45 a.m.; he had several emails to get out before his 9:00 meeting with Randy. One pressing issue was hiring temporary employees for the spike in volume that was anticipated in two weeks. Tammy Larkins was leading the hiring ramp-up and he'd promised her on Friday he would provide feedback on her hiring plan. While reviewing the plan's details, Bill was finding it increasingly hard to stay focused; his mind kept drifting back to his fishing trip with Randy. He was very pleased with Randy's progress to date. He couldn't stop smiling, though he was trying not to get over-confident; Randy wasn't out of the woods yet.

The phone rang and he thought for sure it would be Steve looking for an update on the weekend's activities, but to his surprise it was an unknown number. He debated briefly whether he should answer the phone, or let it roll over to his voicemail.

"Hello, this is Bill Crocoll, how can I help you?"

"Bill, it's Randy. I was wondering if I could stop by a little earlier this morning, say at 8:15? We have a required volume meeting at ten; we're getting ready for the quarter-end push and Fred G. wants to make sure we're all on the same page. Sounds like it could get crazy here! It's the first quarter-end volume push for me, and I'm not sure what to expect, but I'm confident I'm up to the task. I need to be focused on the business, but I also need to run a few things by you, and I don't think an hour will be enough time for you and I to discuss the last three days. Is it possible to move our meeting up forty-five minutes?"

Bill was hesitant. He needed to finish reviewing Tammy's material, and the hiring plan quite frankly was a higher priority for the business than Randy's development, but he was also a little concerned by Randy's comment. Bill's confidence in his progress with Randy took a sudden turn. He thought, *What could have possibly gone wrong?* The smile melted off his face and reality began to sink in again. It crossed his mind that he may have jinxed the process with his overconfidence. "Give me a minute to check my schedule. Is everything going okay for you Randy?"

Randy could tell by the tone of Bill's voice that he was taken aback by his request. "Nothing bad Bill, I just didn't get the results I was looking for with Tom and Rich. I want to spend some time walking through the situation with you. I don't think it's a major setback, but nevertheless, it is a setback for me. I want to discuss my contingency plan with you before I meet with them again. Just want to make sure I have the right bait, and I thought you might have the right lure in your tackle box to use on them."

Bill let out a sigh of relief. "My young friend, you had me a little nervous for a moment there. Don't do that again. Everything seemed to be going so well, I hoped you would have been able to connect this week with Tom and Rich. Don't get discouraged, though; it takes patience to catch fish, and the same concept applies to people. Tom and Rich don't give their respect away easily. If leading people was easy, everyone could do it. I'm interested in hearing what happened with the two of them." Bill checked his day timer and scanned his email for any urgent messages. "8:15 will be fine. See you then."

Bill hung up and immediately dug into Tammy's hiring plan. He didn't want to fix one problem while creating another by getting behind in hiring. He made a few changes to the plan, adjusting the interviewing process map for forklift drivers and adding a few notes on some minor issues. He forwarded the document back to Tammy with his comments and thanked her for a well thought-out plan.

There was a knock at his door. "Come on in, Randy," Bill called. "Though you're a little early."

Bill looked up and was surprised to see Tammy standing at the door.

"You're expecting someone different, Bill?" Tammy said with raised eyebrows. "I wanted to know if you had a chance to review the hiring plan yet." She handed him a printout of the same plan he'd just reviewed. "I have a meeting with Steve at nine. You know Steve better than I do, and I want to make sure I have all my ducks in a row. I really want to gain his confidence that I can deliver."

Bill smiled, understanding Tammy's concern, and asked her to have a seat. "I sure did, Tammy, and overall it's a well thought-out plan. I made a few changes and recommendations for the interviewing process for the forklift drivers. I felt we needed to hire more than you indicated on the plan." Bill pointed to the turnover projection in Tammy's presentation. "I think your projection is about ten percent too low. For this spike, I'd rather be overly cautious. Better to over-hire by ten percent than under-hire, and end up without enough people properly trained and mud on our face." Tammy nodded in agreement. "Other than those two changes, it's good to go. I just hit 'send' on the email, so you should have it when you get back to your office."

Tammy picked up her papers and said, "Great. Thanks for looking at it. I know you have your hands full working with Randy. I'll make those corrections right away."

Bill appreciated Tammy's attention to the details, and wanted her to know he wasn't losing focus on her needs and the challenges she was facing. "Tammy, I appreciate you understanding my situation right now. You're doing a great job flying solo without me. I have all the confidence in the world in you, Tammy. Your meeting with Steve will go just fine. He's a nice guy, very analytical and detail-oriented, but fair. Your plan is well-designed, follows a logical approach, and provides enough details for Steve. Be confident and strong with him. Trust me, he'll like it. Don't waste anymore energy worrying about it, and remember I'm a phone call away."

Tammy could feel the stress subsiding; she knew Steve was a stickler for details, but she really trusted Bill's insight. "I appreciate the vote of confidence. Thanks again for looking it over."

"I want you to know how much I appreciate you taking the lead on this project. I feel bad that I haven't been able to spend time with you lately, but . . ."

Tammy interrupted, "No explanation needed, Bill, I completely understand what you've been working on, and its importance to Steve and the company. Don't worry about it. By the way, how is your special project going?"

Bill thought for a moment. "I think, pretty well so far. I've purposely avoided spending any time on the floor since I started developing him. I didn't want him to think I was checking up on him – I think that would complicate the issues and put additional pressure on him. Have you heard anything?"

Tammy considered Bill's question. "Not really. But I haven't spent much time on the floor in the last few weeks, either. I was walking through yesterday with Tommy Stokes, and things looked good, people seemed happy. From what I could tell, I'd say the plan must be working. My exposure has been very limited, but I think if things weren't getting better, or were even worse, I would have heard about it from someone. Sometimes not hearing anything is a positive sign. Do you want me to reach out to some of my contacts on the floor?"

"No, no, it's not necessary to reach out to anyone; I'm sure if things weren't improving with Randy's performance, you, Steve, or me would have heard something." Bill looked down at his watch and said, "It's ten after eight; you better get running. Steve's a stickler for punctuality."

Tammy stood up, thanked Bill for his time, and left the office. Within minutes, Randy arrived, notebook in hand.

Bill walked around his desk, shook Randy's hand, knowing this was going to be a busy day. "Randy, good morning. You piqued my curiosity with what you said on the phone. Have a seat and update me."

Randy sat down in the chair in front of Bill's desk. "Good morning to you too. No small talk today, huh? You're ready to get down to business."

Bill said, "Sorry about that. I know our time is somewhat limited because of your volume meeting. I want to make sure we have time to cover everything. Let's move over to the table; this seems too formal to me. Would you like a cup of coffee, or some water?"

Randy sat down in the chair across from Bill and opened his notebook. "No, thank you, I just had a cup of coffee." He was grateful for the extra time Bill set aside for him and wanted to make sure to express his appreciation. "Bill, I totally understand the urgency, and appreciate you being able to meet with me earlier than scheduled. So starting with the positives, I think things are going well overall. I'm more relaxed in my role and I believe I'm gaining the confidence of the team." He opened his notebook and continued. "If you'd like an assessment, I have a good connection with sixty-five percent of the team; an average connection with twenty percent of them; ten percent are lukewarm; and then I have Rich and Tom."

Listening to Randy, Bill could see some positive points and wanted to address them right off. "Let me just stop you there. If your assessment is accurate, Randy, I'd say you're doing pretty well, relating very well with the majority of your team. Remember, you'll never make everyone happy, and that shouldn't be your goal. Please continue."

"This is what I'm seeing: the average and lukewarm relationships are moving in the right direction. I'm really focused on the trust issue with all my employees. They're not completely in my camp, but I think they're willing to listen to me and give me a chance. I've been able to gain a very small portion of their confidence. The only concern I have is the amount of time I'm spending trying to win Rich and Tom over. I'm so focused on those two, I worry I'm neglecting other employees."

Bill nodded. "It's a fine line, working out how much time you should spend on any one person or issue. We can discuss the balance of time and relationships later; let's get back to Tom and Rich. On Saturday, you were pretty sure the problem with them was a timing issue. Do you still believe that timing is causing your problem with them?"

Randy shook his head. "It definitely wasn't just the timing. Somehow I think you knew that on Saturday. Just a hunch." Randy smiled. "I've talked to them at several different points during the day, and still no progress. I've tried a different lure every day, and to be honest, I don't have many lures left. My tackle box is running out very quickly. Any thoughts on what I'm doing wrong?"

Bill rubbed his chin and looked out the window. "I don't think you're doing anything wrong with them. I'm impressed you haven't given up. That's a huge improvement in your thought process from a few weeks ago. Do you agree?"

Randy nodded his head. "You're right. I would have blamed them for their behavior and written them off. I'm learning – slowly, but surely."

Bill gave Randy a reassuring look and said, "Randy, you're doing just fine. We just need to keep the ball moving, and things will work out. Okay, let's cover the time balance issue now, before we get into specifics about Rich and Tom. I'm glad you're aware of the time pressure they're putting on you. You have to remember, they're only two members of your team. They're not more important or less important than your other employees, but you can't obsess about winning them over at the expense of the other relationships you've created. You may gain their support, but at the expense of some of the lukewarm relationships on your team."

Randy responded, somewhat confused, "*Obsess* is a strong word, Bill. I'd say *committed,* but I don't think that I'm obsessed with them."

"Okay, I stand corrected: you're committed to, but not obsessed with, building a relationship with them." Bill stood up, took a marker from his desk, and drew a circle on his white board. He turned back to look at Randy. "Randy, please write this down; it's something my mentor taught me. Fish where the fish are."

Randy wrote it down, but looked puzzled. "Fish where the fish are. I'm not sure what that means."

Bill turned back to the white board. "Let me explain. Say you decide to go fishing down at Raynor's pond again. You begin fishing on this side of the pond." Bill drew an X inside the circle on the board.

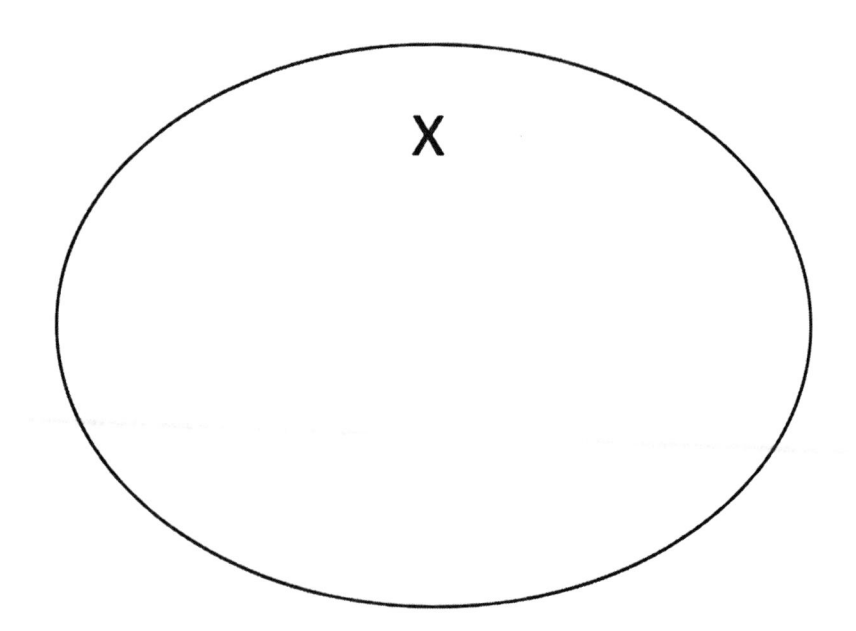

"All morning long, you don't catch any fish. You've changed your bait several times, but no luck. In the afternoon, you switch to the other side of the pond." Bill drew a straight line from the X on the board to the opposite side of the circle. He inserted some crudely drawn fish near the new X.

The People Principles

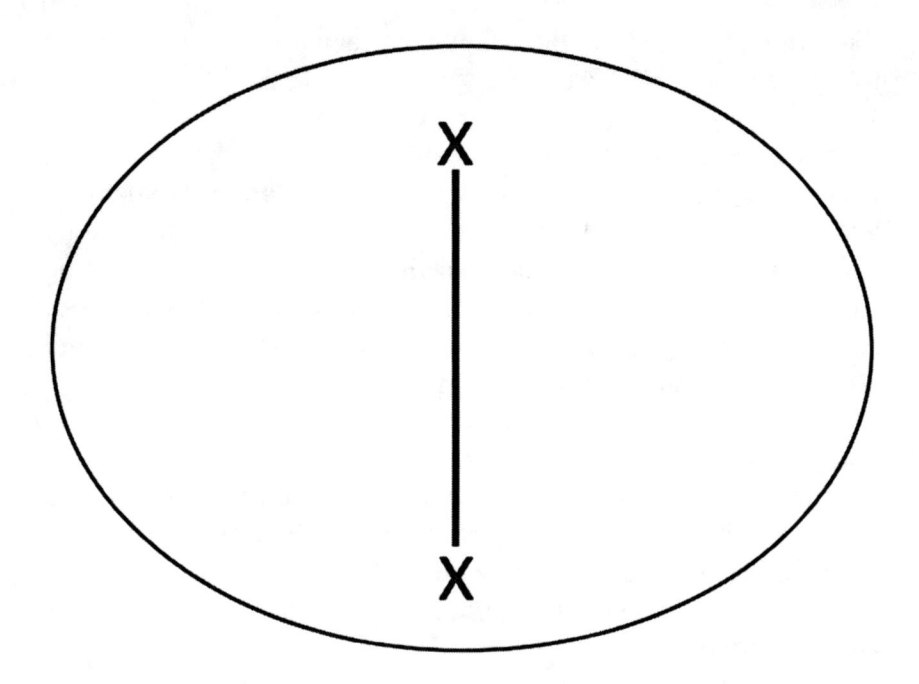

"In the afternoon, you go gangbusters and catch ten fish. Next week, you go fishing again at Raynor's pond. On what side of the pond would you fish?"

Randy stood up and pointed to the second X Bill had put on the board, "I'd fish in the second spot."

"Why there?" Bill asked.

"Because that's where I caught all the fish the week before," replied Randy.

Bill chuckled. "Absolutely. You fish where the fish are, not where the fish aren't. Looking at your team, you have people on your team that are really hitting your bait, you have some folks that are nibbling at it, and you have some people that haven't hit the bait at all. Where should you spend the majority of your time? Where are the fish?"

Randy smiled; he really liked when he could see things coming together. "So what you're saying is to keep fishing with the people that are hitting my lure. How should I deal with the other people, then?"

Bill sat back down and Randy followed. "Keep working on them. Keep changing the bait. Eventually, the hesitation and reluctance will give way to commitment, and most people will come around. If some people don't, you can deal with them later. The one thing to remember is to never give up on those people that you're not connecting with yet. You will be amazed how one little thing – and it can be something so simple – can change a person."

Randy was a little hesitant to agree too quickly that it would be easy gaining the confidence of those who were still reluctant. "That's easier said than done. Let me give you a hypothetical situation, Bill. Suppose you've tried everything humanly possible to win a person over, and he just won't buy into you. Are you saying we should never give up? *Never* is a long time."

Without hesitating, Bill answered, "Never is a long time, but people will amaze you when you least expect it. Let me share a quick story with you. When I first started out, there was this woman working here named Debbie Larson. She and I never hit it off. If I said white, she'd say black. To be honest, I didn't like her. I hate to admit that, but I would avoid her at all costs. I'm sure she didn't like me either. Every interaction with her was a battle, and I had her written off as a lost cause. That's not a great attitude for a Human Resources person, huh?"

Randy smiled briefly and agreed, "It's not a great attitude for anyone to have, but I can relate to it. I'm not at that point with Rich and Tom, but I am getting frustrated with the lack of a positive response from them. Sometimes I want to yell, 'What is wrong with you two guys? Everyone else is getting it!' I definitely can see how you could decide to blow someone off. Did she ever come around, Bill?"

Bill adjusted the blinds on the window so that the morning sun wouldn't be in their eyes. "One day I was in the lunchroom getting a Coke and I saw her on the phone. It was past break time and I was thinking, 'Here we go again.' I waited patiently for her to end her conversation. I was going to write her up for wasting company time. When she finished her call, she was in tears. I was torn between empathy and revenge. To be honest, I was mad that she was crying, because I really wanted to write her up, but I also had a heart."

"Wait a minute," Randy said, with a strange look on his face. "You were mad at her for crying because you couldn't write her up? That shocks me. You really didn't like her."

Bill looked embarrassed at having admitted his pettiness to Randy. "It wasn't my best moment, and I'm not proud of it, but this is the point I want to make. It was a turning point in my career. I was going to let it go, and let her go back to work without saying anything, but I asked her if everything was okay. She was reluctant at first, but she really needed to talk to someone. She was going through a messy divorce. Her husband was pushing for custody of her three children. Her kids were her world, and the thought of losing them was overwhelming. Her story touched my heart; it made me see her in a different light. She wasn't just a pain in the you-know-what any longer; she became a person, in my eyes, with legitimate needs.

"I asked her if she needed anything, and she said she needed to talk to her lawyer ASAP. I brought her up to my office and let her use my phone for twenty minutes. When she was done, she was relieved and couldn't thank me enough. From that point on, our relationship changed completely. I saw her as a person not as a problem that needed to be fixed. It taught me a valuable leadership lesson. Never give up on people, because people can change. Since then, I've never given up on anyone. Which isn't to say there aren't times when I'm tempted to."

Bill could see by the expression on Randy's face that he had a question. "You seem to be struggling with this?" he asked.

Randy looked slightly nervous. "No, I think I get the message, but are you suggesting we never terminate anyone? I can't get my head around that concept. Sometimes people deserve to be terminated."

Bill paused, and then replied, "You're right; some people should and will be terminated from Globalistics. But when people are terminated here, it's not because we've given up on them; it's because they gave up on themselves. We provide employees with regular feedback, we coach them to improve their skills, we develop performance improvement plans to correct deficiencies, and when some employees fail to take advantage of our improvement process, they will eventually be terminated. I always tell people on my team this, and you may want to write this down: I'll provide you with the information, resources, skills, tools, etc.. The only thing I need from you is effort. Some people won't give effort."

Randy was shaking his head, "What a great story, and a great point. I'll continue to fish where there are fish, and I'll keep working on Tom and Rich. Any other approach I should try with them?"

"Thinking about it, the approach may be right, but . . ." Bill took a booklet out of his desk and handed it to Randy. "I want you to take this communication and behavioral assessment, and then we'll go from there. It should only take about fifteen minutes to fill out."

Randy started to flip through the pages. "You didn't say anything about taking a test!"

Bill laughed. "It's not a test! It's an assessment. You'll like it, and it will give great information about yourself and the people on your team."

"If you say so, Bill, I'll believe it's not a test." Randy began filling out the assessment while Bill answered emails. When Randy was finished, he handed it to Bill and asked, "So what does this mean?"

Bill reached into his briefcase and pulled out his iPod. "While I score it, I want you to listen to something. Randy, have you ever been to an opera, or listened to one on a CD?"

The People Principles

Randy gave Bill a strange look. "I grew up on a farm outside Osceola, Iowa. The town has a whooping population of about 500 people. The closest movie theater is forty-five minutes away. So, no, I've never been to an opera, or even listened to one. Opera's not really in my vocabulary. If you said a rodeo or a truck-pull, sure, but an opera? No way." He chuckled and added, "Wait, I did go to the Coldplay concert in Des Moines. Does that count?"

Bill grinned and rolled his eyes. "No, it doesn't count, but I do like their music." Randy raised his eyebrows. "Don't give me that look, I listen to modern music! You'd be surprised at my play list. But today, you're going to listen to *Carmen*. It's my favorite opera. When I'm done looking over this, we can discuss it."

Randy took the iPod and turned it on. "Why do I feel this *Carmen* thing is another step in my development program?"

Bill smiled, happy to see that Randy was learning to be less apprehensive of his development. "You're too suspicious. I'm just trying to broaden your horizons. Giving you a little culture to help you grow outside of your little world, that's it. I believe in total people development," he explained with a laugh.

Bill scored Randy's assessment while Randy listened to the opening aria. Bill could tell by the look on Randy's face that he wasn't enjoying it.

Randy finished with the track and said, with a sly grin, "Sounded great. Got any more?"

Bill looked up, putting down his pencil and turning back to the whiteboard. "Plenty more," he said, and laughed. "We'll cover the assessment first, then your impressions of *Carmen*. Sound like a plan?"

Randy sat back in his chair and said. "Maybe we should cover *Carmen* first; it'll be quick. I didn't understand a word they said. I didn't like it at all."

Bill picked up a marker. "Hold that thought. Let's focus on the assessment. We'll work on adding some culture to your life later. Randy, the assessment places people into four communication and behavioral categories based on how they respond to the questions. The four categories are: directive, engaging, steady, and analyzer." He wrote those four words on the board, making four columns.

Directive	Engaging	Steady	Analyzer

Bill looked at Randy and asked, "Any thoughts on which category you'd fall in to?"

Randy studied the board and answered, "If the assessment is accurate, I have to be an analyzer. At times, I'll fall into an analytical trance. I love crunching numbers. I'm very detail-oriented, and I have a need for order and process. Being analytical is probably my best strength. Am I right?"

Bill knew Randy would process this as he had most of the situations he'd encountered, looking at the surface and not deeper, to the root of the issue. "Not yet; I want to keep you in suspense. Keep in mind, there is no best category. Each one has its advantages and disadvantages. Everyone has communication and behavioral tendencies in each category, but each person has a dominant style.

"The directive individual is very straightforward, with a bottom-line orientation. Out of all the four categories, this person is the most task-oriented and least people-oriented. This doesn't mean they can't be good with people, but they prefer tasks. This person is very focused on achievement; they seek power and prestige, and they have a lot of confidence. They love a variety of activities in their work and personal lives, and love win-lose challenges."

Randy picked up his pen and started writing; he didn't want to forget the categories and their meanings.

Bill gave Randy a minute to finish writing, while he listed several characteristics in the directive column.

Directive	Engaging	Steady	Analyzer
Task-oriented Focus on achievement Seeks power Wants variety Likes to win			

Randy looked at the white board and wrote a few more thoughts. Bill was impressed with Randy's desire to understand these behavioral traits, and continued, "Do you have any directive people on your team?"

Randy looked at the white board and replied, "I know two for sure, Jimmy Kuhn and Truman Bradley. Those two guys are drivers on the floor. You give them an assignment, and get out of their way. They're not afraid to voice their opinions, either. I guess you could classify them as very assertive individuals, maybe even aggressive at times. Would you agree?"

Bill said, "I know them both well. I think you've got them pegged. You could also throw in Dave Ebert." Randy nodded in agreement. "Now let's take a look at the engaging individual. The engager is very gregarious and loves people, is a highly expressive and talkative individual, though a poor listener, and wants democratic relationships. Out of all the communication and behavioral types, this person is the most people-oriented and least task-oriented. This is the big-picture person, not the researcher on the team. This person tends to be disorganized, dislikes detail, is very impulsive, and often thinks with their heart over their mind. Engagers seek popularity and are motivated by recognition from others. Do you have any engagers on your team?" Bill asked as he wrote the engager characteristics on the board.

Directive	Engaging	Steady	Analyzer
Task oriented Focus on achievement Seeks power Wants variety Likes to win	Loves people Expressive Poor listener Disorganized Likes recognition		

Randy finished writing down the information and said, "I think Tom and Rich are engagers. Those guys love to talk, unless it's about numbers or processes. Their forklifts are always messy, and they lose things constantly. I think this week alone, Rich has misplaced or lost his pen four times. It drives me crazy that a grown man can't keep track of his pen. They hate following the process. They like to freelance too much for me. They're definitely engagers."

Bill remembered his own limited interactions with Rich and Tom. "I agree, but you have to admit, people do like them, and overall they're good team players. Hopefully this instrument will help you take advantage of their strengths and minimize their weaknesses."

As Randy wrote in his notebook, he replied, "They do rally the team together, and they're always looking for ways to change things – improve things, actually. Other people on the team love their humor. I just wish they'd cut down on the talk in the aisles and be a little more precise. Usually if we have a miscount, it's in their work. Our cycle count accuracy is 5% below target, and those two guys contribute more to our failure to meet this goal than anyone else."

"I'd have to agree with you, Randy. I haven't spent a ton of time with them, but if I had to take a guess, I'd say they were engagers. Let's talk about the characteristics of a steady person." Bill wrote several characteristics under "Steady" and turned back to Randy, who was already writing.

Directive	Engaging	Steady	Analyzer
Task oriented	Loves people	Likes stability	
Focus on achievement	Expressive	Calm exterior	
Seeks power	Poor listener	Loyal	
Wants variety	Disorganized	Good listeners	
Likes to win	Likes recognition	Don't like change	

"The steady individual is exactly what it sounds like. These people like to have stability in their life, are motivated by security, and are very loyal, to other people and to the company. They're excellent listeners because they're patient; they have trouble meeting multiple deadlines, and seek to maintain the status quo. You can usually tell a steady person by their calm exterior. Two people on your team come to my mind right away; any idea who I'm thinking of?"

Randy looked over the traits, smiled, and answered, "I'd say Molly and Pam."

Bill could see Randy's mind turning. "Those were the two. Why do you think they're steady people, Randy?"

Randy leaned back in his chair. "They're very even-keeled. They really don't get worked up about many things. Their performance and behavior are regular; you pretty much know what you're going to get from them every day. The only criticism I would have is they can be territorial with their area. They don't like other people nosing around their work. Now I understand why they became so upset when I tried to change the inventory process. It was more than me not getting them involved in the decision, though I understand that didn't help the situation. But they also wanted to maintain the status quo."

Bill nodded. "Great application of the steady category to Pam and Molly. When you're making changes with steady people, the change needs to be planned and well-communicated. Give me a second and let me fill in the analyzer category." Bill begin writing in the remaining column, while Randy continued copying the chart into his notebook.

Directive	Engaging	Steady	Analyzer
Task oriented Focus on achievement Seeks power Wants variety Likes to win	Loves people Expressive Poor listener Disorganized Likes recognition	Likes stability Calm exterior Loyal Good listeners Don't like change	Precise/ methodical Analytical Detail oriented Impatient Trouble delegating Perfectionist

Bill pointed to the fourth column. "Okay, this person is very precise, methodical, and sees things in black and white. They're detail-oriented, stubborn, and don't always delegate well. They take great pride in the exactness of their work, and they love information; they're great researchers, but can overanalyze at times. Do you still think you're an analyzer?"

When Randy finished writing, he looked up and answered without hesitating, "Without a doubt, that's me through and through. I have a bit of the directive characteristic, too. I'm not sure if that's a good combination or not, but I'm sure you'll tell me."

Bill smiled. "I'm very impressed with your self-assessment. You're a very strong analyzer, but with a high score in the directive category as well. We call your profile the horseshoe pattern. Many of our senior leaders have horseshoe patterns, so you're in good company." Bill paused for a moment. "I'm proud of you; most people don't know the type of person they are."

"Bill, I'd love to say it was a lucky guess, but I only recognized it as you explained the assessment to me. Taking the time to write down each of the behavioral traits and matching them up with associates

I lead makes it very real and insightful. Now that I'm gaining a better understanding of my behavioral type, what does this all mean to me?"

Bill stood silent for a moment as Randy looked up at him. "We'll get back to the assessment in a minute. We need a little break. Tell me what you thought of the opera."

Randy laughed. "You're kidding me, right? You tell me what I am, but you're not going to tell me what it means. Something about that just doesn't make sense."

Bill walked back over to the table and sat down, smiling. "Randy, your style is coming out now: no patience. We'll get back to the assessment in a minute, but let's talk about *Carmen*."

Randy put his pen down and crossed his arms. "All right, but you know me. I want the details. Let me see. *Carmen*. Like I said, I didn't understand a word they sang. What language was it, anyway?"

"It was French. I take it you don't speak or understand French?"

"No, I've never studied French. I took two years of German in high school, and I don't even remember much of that. I can say hello, goodbye, count to ten, and ask where the bathroom is. Would you like to hear some?"

Smiling, Bill said, "We can save your German for another day. So you didn't understand a word of the music? Because you don't speak French, you couldn't understand the opera. Remember that point for later." He gestured back toward the white board. "Getting back to the assessment, can you see from the characteristics on the board and in our discussion that each of those individuals has different communication styles and behaviors?"

Randy was confused; he was trying to figure out where Bill was going with this conversation, and it wasn't making sense to him. "You're losing me here, boss."

Bill acknowledged Randy's bewilderment with a smile. "I don't mean to confuse you, but it will make more sense to you in a minute. Now look at the board."

Randy examined the board and some of his notes. "I'd guess that people in each category probably see the world a little differently. They're motivated by different factors. I think I get it. I have to use a different leadership style with each of the different type of individuals. We discussed this concept last week."

Bill could sense Randy becoming a little frustrated with the direction of the conversation. "We did discuss it last week. You're right that leaders have to use different styles with each of the different types of people, but there's more to it. We also have to use different languages."

Randy looked confused; he was trying to follow Bill, but it wasn't making sense yet. "We have to use different languages," he repeated. "Bill, help me out here for a minute. I'm only fluent in English, and to the best of my knowledge, everyone on the team is fluent in English as well. I'm not seeing that I have a language barrier with my team."

Bill continued pushing. "Everyone does speak and understand English on the team, but I'm not talking about native language. I'm talking about category language. You look lost."

Randy shook his head slowly back and forth and said, "I am lost. I'm not sure what you're talking about. What do you mean *category language?*"

"Let's use a real-life example. You identified Rich and Tom as engagers." Randy nodded and Bill continued, "The assessment identified you as an analyzer. Now look at both of those categories. Do you see any differences between them?"

Randy paused as he examined the board, "The one difference I see right away is the attention to detail. The engager isn't detailed-oriented and is disorganized, while the analyzer is very detailed-oriented and organized. Those two categories are almost complete opposites."

Bill interjected, "They are different, but they can complement each other, when the approach and language is correct."

Randy broke in, his tone puzzled. "I'm trying to follow you, but I don't understand this language thing. I can see the behavioral piece, but Tom and Rich speak and understand English very well. I don't see your point."

Bill leaned back in his seat and hesitated before trying again. "Randy, you told me this week that you tried two or three times to connect with Rich and Tom. You talked about the department's needs, strengths, weaknesses, and your vision for the team, and you didn't think it went well. What you're trying apparently isn't working for you. Tell me how the discussion went."

"Let's see." Randy closed his eyes and tilted his head backwards. "Not sure if I can get it exactly word for word, but I'll paraphrase as closely as possible. I shared the index report, and went into great detail with the numbers. I wanted them to understand the areas where we were knocking it out of the park, and a few areas needing improvement. I covered the picking and loading processes in detail to illustrate where they were breaking down, and what we could do to improve them. I gave them feedback on their need to improve their accuracy. Finally, I discussed my development plan for the team. I'm going to talk one about of our measurements each Friday at our shift meeting; I want to explain what the measurement is, how we get the data, the formula used to derive the number, and what it's used for. It was great information, but they asked very few questions. They didn't seem interested in discussing it, which surprised me. Who wouldn't be interested in our team measurements? I think that's about the extent of the discussions. Don't you think that was all pertinent information?"

Bill nodded, pen flying to capture Randy's summary on his notepad.

"It's information they need, and that the team needs as well. The unfortunate thing is that Tom and Rich didn't understand it. To them it was like you listening to *Carmen*. You didn't understand a word of the opera, and they didn't understand when you were talking to them. Each category speaks a different *type* of English. Let me play back what you communicated to them. Listen carefully to the words you used and look at the board. This is how you'd describe the conversation: 'I went into great detail, and I covered the picking and loading processes in detail. I shared the formula to derive the number.'"

Randy felt himself growing defensive. "Bill, I went slow, I spoke on their level, and I explained everything in detail. I had to go into a lot of detail, because the measurements are difficult to understand. It wasn't a language issue. It was their attitudes. They don't want to understand it. It's is amazing to me that they understand each other, when they're out there in the aisle talking instead of working."

The tension in room was palpable. Bill took a deep breath and said carefully, "Randy, you're taking this personally now. It's not a personal attack on you. Look at the board again. When you spoke to them, did you speak from *your* category or *their* category? Do you see anything in their category about details?"

Feeling the tension as well, Randy adjusted himself in his seat and made a conscious effort to relax and be objective. He carefully looked at the board, then his notes, and then closed his eyes, replaying the conversation with Rich and Tom. He opened his eyes. "I get that engagers aren't detailed-oriented. I spoke from my language category, not theirs. But how do I speak from a language category if I'm not in it?"

Bill sensed a breakthrough. "You don't have to be in it, Randy. You just have to understand it, and be able to communicate so they understand you. Each of these categories not only has behavioral tendencies, but a separate language as well. The problem is that people get comfortable speaking their own language, and don't try to speak the language of the person they're talking to. But you have to remember: it's not what you say, it's what the other person hears. Clear as mud yet?"

Randy grabbed his pen and started writing again, not wanting to forget how it all came together. He remembered that back in school, the instructor would bring all the details of a lesson together and he would finally see what they were saying, but later, it was never as clear.

Randy put his pen down and said, a little dejected, "Leadership is really hard. There's so much to know. I always thought English was English, but now you're telling me you need to use the right type of English for the type of person you're talking to. Wait until I tell them about this back on the farm." Both Randy and Bill laughed. "The fact is, Rich and Tom didn't get engaged in the conversation. Now I'm seeing that they don't like details, and I'm hammering them with details. I was speaking my language, not theirs. But Bill, they need to understand the numbers to be more effective on the job. Man, I'm really lost. Can you show me how I could have communicated the same message in their language?"

Bill gave Randy a reassuring smile. "Sure thing, Randy, let's role-play the situation. I'll be you and you can be Tom – he's better-looking than Rich."

Randy laughed. For the next thirty minutes, Randy and Bill role-played. After Bill role- played being Randy, he gave Randy the chance to role-play the situation as himself.

When Randy finished, Bill had feedback for him. "Very nice job, Randy. I want to caution you, though, even if you speak their language, it's going to take a continued effort to connect with them. There isn't any leadership shortcut, magic pill, or pixy dust that works with people, but I believe this will give you the best chance to make things work. When you're dealing with people, nothing is guaranteed. We don't come with a set of directions: insert four D batteries and turn on. But you'd better run to your meeting; you only have five minutes."

Randy quickly wrote a few final points in his notebook and stood up. "Too bad we don't come with instructions; it would make leadership so much easier. Once again, thanks for your time Bill."

"No problem. Give me a call after your meeting to schedule our next one-on-one."

Randy hurried out of the office and Bill began checking his voicemails and emails. Within fifteen minutes, Bill was startled to see Randy standing at his door again. "Did you forget something?"

Randy was out of breath. "No," he said, and inhaled deeply. "The meeting was pushed back to one o'clock. Do you have a few minutes?"

Bill looked at his watch. "I can give you five minutes. I have a meeting with Dennis Moore, and you don't keep him waiting. Most impatient man I've ever met. Is it quick?"

"Pretty quick. I've been working with Brian on his development, and I've spent lots of time with him but I'm not seeing any results. Zero progress to date. I'd like to discuss it with you before I meet with him again on Monday."

Bill thought for a moment. "We have a lunch date with Nick on Saturday. I'm planting my vegetable garden that morning; would you like to come out to the house, and you can talk while I work?"

Randy chuckled. "I would love to see you do some physical labor for once. I'll bring my video camera, just to show everyone you do actually sweat." He grinned at Bill's raised eyebrows. "I'm just kidding, I know you work hard. I'd love to come out; maybe I can help you plant. What time should I come over?"

Bill looked at his watch and grabbed some papers, "Nine o'clock at my place. See you then. I need to run." He patted Randy on the shoulder and walked briskly toward Steve's office.

Chapter Eight
Green Beans

Bill was sitting on his deck, enjoying a cup of coffee before he got to work in the garden. It was one of those beautiful spring mornings: not a cloud in the sky, low humidity, perfect temperature. His yard backed up to a large wooded field filled with maple trees and wildflowers. Many mornings he would awaken to a handful of deer grazing in the flowers. Casey had grown up in western Kentucky, and the location of their home was a compromise: he was a city boy and she was a country girl. It was located within the city limits for him, but had the touch of country that Casey wanted. As Bill gazed aimlessly toward the woods admiring the beautiful day, he worked through a mental checklist of everything needed to sow the garden.

"Hey, honey, you look like you're in pretty deep thought for so early on a Saturday," said Casey, sitting down next to Bill on the deck. She was wearing her favorite pink and white polka-dot half-robe that Bill bought her.

Bill reached over and took Casey's hand, giving it a gentle squeeze. "I know I say it every year, but spring really is my favorite season. The flowers in bloom, the grass, the leaves coming in on the trees – it renews the spirit. I just love it. It's a great day to be alive, though then again, every day is a great day to be alive. Oh, before I forget, remember I'll be having lunch today at Nick's house with Randy. I promise, tonight I am all yours."

"Well, I'm glad you can squeeze me into your day." Bill began to reply, but Casey smiled at him and said, "Honey, please don't worry about it, I know how important this project is to you. Besides, when you finish with Randy, I'll probably be able to talk you into putting in my gazebo." They both laughed and Casey asked, "What time are you meeting Randy at Nick's house?"

Casey's question caught Bill off guard; he thought he'd told her that Randy would be coming by the house that morning. "Oh boy, didn't I tell you that Randy's coming here first? We're going to drive over to Nick's together. I told him to be here by nine. Is that a problem, sweetheart?"

Bill could tell by the look on Casey's face that he definitely hadn't told her. Casey put her hand on Bill's leg and said with a cute grin, "So now I'm 'sweetheart'! No, you never mentioned that detail to me, my dear. Nine o'clock – why is he coming over so early? Lunch isn't until 11:45, I thought."

Bill took a sip of coffee. "He's going to help me plant the garden. You know, he grew up on a farm in Iowa and can probably give me some good tips. I'm going to win the tomato competition with Larry this year."

Casey leaned back in her chair, folded her arms, and chuckled, "Bill Crocoll, I can't believe you've tricked Randy into helping you with the garden, disguising it as part of his development plan. I don't believe you sometimes."

Bill laughed and set his cup down on the table, not about to let her get away with that accusation. "First of all, he volunteered, and secondly, it *is* a part of his development plan. I've got a great learning point for him today. You know I'd never just take advantage of someone for free labor."

Casey looked at Bill with a smile on her face. "I'm sure you have something planned for him with the garden, and I don't mind Randy coming by the house. I just wish you'd have told me about it last night. I would have gotten up earlier so I could be put together when he arrives. I need to be dressed and have my makeup on before I meet him." She got up from her chair and straightened her robe. "I'm looking forward to meeting the person you've been spending so much time with lately, but I'd better get in the shower before your 'volunteer' arrives. To think, you market yourself as a communication guru." She laughed and headed toward the door.

Bill roared after her, "I am a communication *expert*, and I didn't trick him either! He wanted to help!"

He finished his cup of coffee and headed to the garage to get the tools, soil, and plants and seeds for the garden. He'd bought some rich soil with special nutrients for this year's garden. He and his neighbor Larry had an ongoing, friendly competition to see who could grow the largest tomato. This year he was committed to winning it.

Working in the yard and planting his garden each year gave Bill a feeling of pioneer spirit; he thoroughly enjoyed being able to grow food in his backyard for his family. Besides, there was nothing better to him than home-grown tomatoes, spinach, corn, and green beans. As he was loading the soil into the wheelbarrow, Randy drove up to the house in his truck and parked it in the driveway. "Hold on there, I'll give you a hand with all your stuff," Randy shouted as he got out of his truck. "I don't want you to hurt yourself; we have a big day ahead of us."

Bill replied merrily, "Hey, Randy. I thought you were going to be a blister today and show up after the work was done."

Randy laughed as he shook Bill's hand. "Planting a backyard garden is like a day at the beach for this old farm boy. To be honest with you, I enjoy this stuff."

Bill patted Randy on the back and pointed towards the house. "Make sure you tell my wife that; she thinks I tricked you into helping me today. If you'll grab the shovel and hoe, I'll push the wheelbarrow out back."

Randy and Bill took the soil and tools to the backyard garden. As they were walking toward the back of the house, Randy asked, "Am

I going have to the chance to meet your wife today? I'd like to see your better half."

Bill smiled. "Yeah, she's in the house getting ready, and she wants to meet you as well. She takes a little longer to get ready than I do, but she looks ten times better than I do when she's done."

Randy nodded. "Great; I'm really looking forward to meeting her. Based on what you've told me about her, she sounds like an amazing person. Does your wife work outside of the home?"

"Yes, she does work outside the home. But most people would ask, 'Does your wife work?' – your parents raised you right. She's been teaching middle school history for the last three years. I'm really proud of her. She was a stay-at-home mom until Ralston, Markus, and MacKensey finished high school. Then she finished her degree, and now she works at Dunkirk Middle School. She loves it. Here she comes. Hey, babe, this is Randy Sysol. Randy, this is my wife Casey." Casey had two bottles of water in her left hand for Bill and Randy.

They both smiled as she approached; Casey reached out and shook Randy's hand with a grip that matched his. "Randy, it's nice to meet you. I've heard so many good things about you from Bill. He tells me you grew up on a farm in Iowa. I'm a country girl from Kentucky. Someday we need to sit down and talk about our farming experience." Casey handed the water bottles to Bill and Randy; both said, "Thank you."

Randy smiled and told her, "That would be great. I'm sure we have some of the same fond memories – and not so fond ones – from being raised on a farm." He looked over at Bill and added, "I want you to know, your husband is an amazing man."

Casey looked at Bill and answered, "I think so too. Glad you could come over and help Bill with his garden."

"The garden – yeah, I didn't know we'd be gardening until I got here today." Casey's eyes opened wide and Randy hastened to say, "Just kidding, just kidding, I volunteered to help out." Everyone laughed. "Are you going to join us? I'd love to get to know you better."

Casey shook her head. "I think I'll leave the fun to you boys. I talked our daughter Kensey into going to a craft show with me today. It was nice to meet you, Randy. Have fun – and I think you're really going to enjoy your lunch with Nick. He's a neat person."

"It was nice to meet you as well." Randy shook Casey's hand and Bill kissed his wife goodbye.

Randy looked at Bill and said, "Bill, your wife is great! You can see the passion and energy in her. I just met her, but I can tell she's a great person. I bet the kids at school love her."

"I'm a lucky man. To be honest, there are many times when I look at her, and I can't believe she's my wife." Bill paused as he watched Casey walk into the house. "Not sure what she saw in me, but I'm sure glad she did. Well, let's get this garden planted so we can get to Nick's on time."

Randy and Bill spread the soil in the garden and began with the tomato plants. Bill wanted three rows of tomato planted on the top half of the garden. As Randy dug the hole for each starter, Bill handed him the plant.

"Any progress with Rich and Tom this week?" asked Bill.

Randy hesitated as he judged whether the hole he'd dug was deep enough for the tomato plan. "I wouldn't call it progress, but I can't say it was a setback, either. I'm still working with them, but they're not buying into my vision for the team. They're just not excited about it like the other folks. Not sure what's wrong with them. They don't seem to see the future."

Bill reached for some more soil for his tomato plant. "Hmmm. Do they understand your team's goals and objectives, what's required for your vision?"

Randy stopped planting for a moment and answered with conviction, "Absolutely. I've made sure everyone on the team understands the work standards for their job." Before Bill could say anything, Randy went on. "All the standards have been posted in the department, and in my one-on-ones with them, we discuss how they're performing against them. Rich and Tom definitely know what the job requirements are for their position. It's something else. I just haven't connected with them yet."

"Randy, work standards and team goals are totally different. Work standards are the day-to-day work requirements necessary to meet the needs of the business. Goals are incremental targets required to achieve the team's vision. Do you see the difference?"

Randy stopped spreading the soil for a moment as he thought about Bill's question. "Not really. I don't see much difference at all between them. Goals are different from standards? Can you explain it in more detail?"

"I will, but I have one more question. You know where you want to take the team in the future. Do you know where your team is today?"

"Today we're performing okay, but obviously we can do better. That's what I'm preaching daily. When we do better as a team, it's better for them individually. Everybody wins in my equation. Trust me Bill, we'll get there."

Bill liked to see the confidence Randy had in his team. "I like your philosophy, that everybody wins, but your team needs a roadmap to get there. It's one thing to say it, but another thing to do it. The road to success starts with understanding where your team is right now. Have you ever used MapQuest?"

Randy laughed. "You always have interesting questions. I use it all the time; why?"

"What are the two pieces of information you need to get directions from MapQuest?" asked Bill.

"You need to have a starting point and a destination," responded Randy.

Bill clapped Randy on the shoulder. "Correct. If you don't have a starting point, can MapQuest provide you with directions to your destination?"

"No, the system needs a starting point so it can map out the correct route."

"It's the same thing with your team, Randy: you and the team need a starting point to map out your future." Bill used his hands to illustrate his example. "Without a starting point, the team may not understand the need for the change, or the steps to get where you want them. Those steps are your goals. On Monday, come by the office and I'll give you an instrument to assess your team. I would have everyone on the team complete the assessment confidentially, and have Molly collect them and tabulate the results for you. This will help give you and your team a starting point."

"Sounds good. I'll stop by your office first thing and get moving on it." Cradling a tomato plant in his hands, he added, "I'm starting to get it now. I've been so focused on where we need to go, I haven't given them a picture of where they are today. People need to understand why they need to change, rather than just changing for the sake of change."

Bill nodded his head in total agreement. "Very good. It's very important to be able to distinguish the present situation from goals for the future, to understand why and how you need to change. Let me explain the difference between work standards and goals. First, you must understand the difference between a group of people and a team. A team works toward a common goal, which provides the team with purpose. A group works to meet job standards. Where a group fails to become a team is at the level of commitment. The only way to get team commitment is by providing them with a mission, vision, goals, and objectives. This creates a sense of common purpose, and that common purpose leads to commitment. Commitment creates high morale, and high morale usually results in high productivity. Make sense to you?"

By now Randy was sitting back in the grass, his full attention on Bill. He answered less confidently, "Sort of, but I'd think that if everyone knew their productivity standards, and everyone hit their goals, we'd be hitting our KPI's with or without a mission or vision. Missions and vision statements sound pretty abstract to me. Not sure if my team would buy into it right now." Randy shrugged his shoulders. "They'd probably think it was some college thing. I need to get them past the school-boy stereotype."

Bill thought for a moment and then responded, "You're probably right for short term results, but we're not focused on short term results here; we want the employees of Dunkirk Distribution and Globalistics to achieve long-term success." Bill paused to let Randy think about his statement. "You and your team will never reach the potential each of you have without knowing who you are today as a team, and where you want to go in the future. Purposeless teams fall into complacency, plain and simple. Mission and vision statements provide teams with a sense of direction and purpose. People need purpose in their life, don't they?"

Hesitantly Randy said, "I'm sure you're right." He sat facing Bill with a blank stare.

Bill sized up the situation. He could see that Randy was struggling with the concepts of mission and vision. He stood up, rubbed his hands together to get some of the soil off, and took a deep breath before he started to explain. "Randy, this is one of my core values. I truly believe in having a mission and vision for everything I do. I know what it's done for my team. You're not the only person at Dunkirk Distribution who struggles with it. We have several leaders with years of experience that have a hard time buying into the necessity of developing a mission and vision statement." Bill could tell that

The People Principles

Randy was listening intently to every word. "I've talked until I'm blue in the face with a couple of them. I feel sorry for them, and really feel sorry for the people working for them. Some of them are successful, but I truly believe they will never reach their full potential, because of their failure to provide their team with purpose and direction. But it's critical for people to have a purpose. Do you agree with that, Randy?"

Randy didn't need to think about his reply; he believed strongly in the need for a purpose. "Yeah, I do believe that people need purpose or direction in their life. I think it gives meaning on many different levels."

"Let me share a story with you." Bill took a sip of water; Randy opened his bottle and did the same. "The summer after I had graduated with my bachelor's degree, and before I started working on my Master's, I needed to find a job. The economy was poor and it was a tough market. I was lucky to find a job with the City of Dunkirk in the public maintenance department. On my first day, my boss drove me to a green vacant field. During the drive over, he asked me a bunch of questions about myself, typical small talk. He didn't mention anything we'd be doing that morning. When we got to the field he told me to grab the shovel out of the bed of the pick-up truck and follow him. I picked up the shovel, and we walked about twenty-five yards out into the middle of the field. He told me to dig a hole twelve inches by twelve inches, and sixteen inches deep. Out of all the holes that I ever dug in my life, it was the best. When I finished digging, I proudly asked my boss, Dave Bradnick, to come and inspect it. I thought he would praise my effort, but instead he told me to fill it back in with dirt."

Randy interrupted, "Wait a second, he told you to fill the hole back in with dirt? What was the point of digging the hole in the first place? That doesn't make any sense at all. Now that would make me mad."

Bill took another sip of his water; Randy was so engrossed in the story that he forgot to drink. "I'll get to that. After I filled the hole back in with dirt, he took me five more yards out in the field and told me to dig another hole. I dug that hole and he told me the same thing, to fill it back in with dirt. After that he had me dig three more holes, and each time, you know what he told me?"

"Let me guess: to fill them back in with dirt."

Bill smiled broadly. "Yep, he had me fill them back in with dirt. After filling in the fifth hole, I told him I felt like an idiot, digging holes and then, was I was done, filling them up again. It didn't make any sense to me, and I was becoming frustrated with the task, basically feeling and looking stupid because there was no point to it. He rubbed his face and apologized. He thought he'd told me what we were doing: the next day, the city was bringing in heavy equipment to do major digging in the field, and there was a water pipe running through it that we needed to find, so they wouldn't break it. Once I knew the purpose of digging the holes, it was motivating. It was a challenge to find the needle in the haystack. My work had a purpose."

Randy sat back with an amazed look on his face. "I totally didn't see where you were going with the story – I was just confused as to why anyone would ask an employee to dig a hole and fill it back up again. I get the point, though. People need a purpose and a goal, to understand what their task or job is meant to accomplish.

Bill clapped his hands together and said, "Exactly. You'll never have a team unless you provide them with goals to give them purpose. A team needs to know what their goals are in order to achieve their vision. Let's discuss your team's goals."

Randy outlined his three-year plan for his team, including a lot of detail to explain the yearly goals and objectives needed to accomplish his vision.

"Randy, that sounds great," Bill told him. "What you need to do is cover all that with your team on Monday." He looked at his watch and added, "We need to hurry and plant these green beans, or we'll be late for lunch. Grab those two stakes and the string."

Randy picked up the string. "What do you want me to do with this?"

Bill winked and assured him, "I have a few planting tricks up my sleeve. Hand me one of those stakes; you take the other one and stick it in the ground in front of you. Then tie the string to your stake and bring the string to me, and I'll tie it to my stake. The string will give us a straight line to plant the green bean seeds."

Randy laughed. "Bill, I'm impressed with your method. I haven't ever seen this before – it's not bad for a city slicker."

"I'll show you city slicker," Bill chuckled. "Actually, I read about this in one of my wife's gardening magazines. If the seeds are planted in a straight line, it helps them grow bigger and produce more beans."

Randy was enjoying his time outdoors, and the insight he was gaining from Bill was extremely helpful. There was another issue he wanted to discuss, and he thought this would be a good time. "Bill, while we're planting, let me tell you about my frustration with Brian. You know he wants to be developed into an inventory control person, rather than in a maintenance role, which is where we have him now. We developed a plan together, and we've discussed a portion of it almost every day, but I haven't seen any progress from him. I don't understand it, because I'm also developing Phyllis Barone in cycle counting, and she's doing great. I can see her growing every day, unlike Brian. Brian's an analyzer so I know I'm using the right language with him; I'm just not getting any results. What do you think?"

"Give me a minute. Hmmm. Did I ever tell you about the first time I planted a garden?"

Randy thought for a moment. "I don't think so; you just told me how much you enjoyed it."

"It was about four years ago. I was admiring my neighbors' garden and thought it would be neat to have my own. I discussed the idea with Casey, and she said go for it. I did pretty much the same thing we're doing today. I planted the green beans, watered the seeds, and went to bed that night with great anticipation. When the sun came up I jumped out of bed, put my robe on and ran to the garden. I got out here, and you know what I saw?"

Randy smirked. "You probably saw wet dirt. You can't expect immediate results; the beans weren't going to grow overnight. Crops take time and patience, Bill. I hate to say this, but if you thought you would have green beans the next day, you were green."

Both men laughed as Bill replied, "I learned that concept very quickly. Every day I would check the garden for progress. I'd water daily to keep the seeds moist. I knew I had to continue nurturing them in order for them to grow. If I didn't water the seeds, what would happen to them?"

Randy knew the answer from his years of farming with his family. "If you didn't continue to take care of the seeds, they'd dry up and die. Your garden wouldn't produce anything."

"Not bad for a country boy," smiled Bill. "Within a few weeks I saw my first sprouts. It was great. I got the whole family out to the garden, took pictures, and bragged. I was so proud and excited about my initial success, but could I stop watering and taking care of the beans now?"

Randy quickly replied, "Absolutely not! The sprouts still needed water, and the garden would need to go on being weeded if you wanted the plants to produce beans."

Bill nodded. "Exactly. So I continued to care for the garden, and I soon noticed that some plants were growing faster than others. Some were taller and stronger, while others were slower and smaller. Should I have pulled those ones out?"

Randy took a sip of his water and gave Bill a skeptical look. "Why would you pull the smaller plants out? They're still good plants."

Bill nodded again. "You're right. I continued to care for all the plants, large and small. I was amazed that some of the smaller plants eventually outgrew the larger plants and actually produced more green beans. Some of them needed more care and water than others, but eventually all of them grew into mature plants and produced good results. That first season of growing green beans, I learned a lot not only about growing vegetables, but also about people. Most leaders are doers. They're given a task, get it done right away, see immediate results, and are rewarded for their accomplishments. Do you consider yourself a doer?"

Randy responded almost immediately, "Yes, I'm a doer. I like getting things done. I think one of my strengths is my sense of urgency; give me a task and get out of my way. I love mowing grass – I like seeing with every pass around the yard the progress that I'm making. My problem is that I don't have patience for people that lack that sense of urgency. It drives me crazy."

Bill took another sip of his water. "You are a doer. The one thing that I hear more than anything else about you is your strong work ethic and your passion for results. Those are both very positive attributes to have as a leader. But another key characteristic of leadership is patience, especially when you're developing people on your team. Remember what you told me when I got up on the first day and didn't see any progress in my garden?"

Randy paused to recall his previous comment. "Yeah, you can't expect immediate results. It requires time and patience, and then more patience, to grow crops. You can't expect green beans to grow overnight."

Bill smiled and looked directly at Randy. "Exactly. The same principles apply to people. You can't expect people to grow overnight. It takes time and patience. I worked in the garden every day, nurturing and cultivating the green beans, and for a while, I didn't see any results. But I believed that if I was diligent with my care, the plants would eventually grow, and they did, and produced beans. I didn't see any immediate results but I believed in their potential to grow. Right now, you're developing two people. One person is growing faster than the other, right?"

"Phyllis is growing, and I'm not seeing any growth with Brian. I need to keep watering Brian, don't I?"

Again Bill nodded. "I think so. See, some people will start to grow immediately, some need more water and care than and some people will eventually grow bigger and produce more than others as well. Remember, just because you haven't seen Brian growing on the outside, doesn't mean he's not growing on the inside. You have to believe in people like I believed in the green beans. I watered the seeds every day even though I couldn't see the visible growth until they sprouted. But I believed that they were growing under the soil. Is it possible that Brian is growing on the inside, and just hasn't sprouted yet?"

"That's the part I can't be certain about, at least not yet. I do believe he's committed to the plan, and I want to believe that if I continue to work with him, he'll sprout and produce results."

Bill looked at his watch. "One last point. Remember, some people may grow slower in the beginning, but in the long run will out-produce others who grew faster in the beginning. Sometimes we make assumptions about people, because one person gets out of the gate faster than another, and so we immediately think this person is a better performer. But in the long run, the slower person out performs the quick starter. I'm not saying this is the case with Brian and Phyllis, but you won't know until you've completed their development plans."

Randy was soaking up the ideas. "I need to remember that development takes time, and results aren't always immediate. And you developed this concept from growing green beans. Simply amazing!"

Bill put up a finger. "I have one thing to add. With most people, development isn't usually visible for a while. If you keep watering, nurturing, and cultivating people, they'll grow, and most will surprise you with what they can accomplish. People never cease to amaze me." Bill looked at his watch. "Man, this morning is flying by. Let's get all the tools back to the garage and get cleaned up. Nick is expecting us in forty-five minutes."

Randy started putting the tools back into the wheelbarrow. "Bill, I have to be honest with you. I wasn't sure Brian was worth investing much time in. But after you told me about Debbie Larson, and not giving up on people, and now with the green bean story about nurturing and patience, I'm starting to agree with everything you said this morning. I need to continue working on Brian's development. Hopefully he'll eventually reveal his progress to me. If he doesn't, it won't be because I wasn't patient, or that I gave up on him."

Bill pushed the wheelbarrow while Randy walked beside him. Once they had hung the tools back up in the garage, Bill invited Randy into the house to clean up, and then they headed to Nick's house.

Chapter Nine
Milk Bones

Bill and Randy drove to Nick's, admiring the beauty of the country setting and rolling hills of Western New York. It brought Randy a sense of peace and warmth, reminding him of his hometown. He was amazed by the amount of grapes grown in the area. The vineyards went on for miles. The terrain was very similar to the hills of Iowa, but the agriculture was strikingly different. When Randy would take a relaxing drive through Iowa, he'd see corn and soy beans and more corn and soy beans; those were the crops Iowa was known for.

They arrived at Nick's house exactly at 11:45, and were greeted in the driveway by Nick, who was walking towards them, looking at his watch. "Bill, I could set the clocks by you; here you are, right on time. I should have known, of course – not only are you on time for appointments, but you're definitely on time for a meal." All of them laughed out loud and shook hands. Nick asked how the planting had gone.

Bill told him, "It went great. Got everything in, and this year with my special soil I'm sure to win the tomato contest with my neighbor. It's definitely going to be my year!"

Nick winked at Randy and smiled. "My question was actually for Randy. I knew *you* would be excited about it. Apparently, you managed to sucker this young man into helping you with your chores. I don't know how you talk people into some things."

Bill threw both of his hands shoulder high and said, "Hold on, Nick, Casey accused me of the same thing this morning. I want to set the record straight once and for all. I didn't sucker him into helping me;

he volunteered his labor this morning. Now Randy, tell Nick you came over willingly to help out today."

Looking askance at Bill, Randy turned toward Nick and put his hand next to his mouth so Bill couldn't see what he was saying. He whispered, "I have no idea what he's talking about." Nick let out a loud laugh and Bill just glared at Randy. Randy grinned and said, "Come on, Bill, I had to give you a little bit of a hard time. Nick, honestly, while we were in Bill's office he told me he was going to be working in his garden, and I volunteered to help. It was fun. I've been away from my parent's farm for a few years now, and it was good to get my hands in the soil again. I had the chance to meet Casey; she's a great lady. It gave Bill and me an opportunity to talk, about work and about other things. Plus, I did get a chance to ask a few questions about an employee issue I'm dealing with at work. So really, I got the better end of the deal."

Nick smiled at Bill and said, "You really planned this well." Randy laughed and Nick continued, "So, you got a chance to meet Casey. Definitely Bill's better half . . . "

Bill said, "My, Nick, you're really out to get me today – although you're right; I'm a very lucky man."

Nick smiled. "OK. Enough picking on Bill. Randy, if you don't mind me asking, what's the employee issue you're dealing with at work?"

Randy looked at Bill, then back at Nick, and replied, "I don't mind at all. I'm developing an employee, and I'd been feeling like the plan wasn't very productive. I didn't see any immediate measurable or observable results. So Bill helped me work through the issue, and used a great analogy of growing green beans and developing people. Did he ever tell you about that one?"

Nick smiled at Bill. "Yes, he did. Bill's a deep thinker, and I'm always amazed at how he can take something as basic as planting green beans and relate it to his job, or people generally. It's a gift. And it's a brilliant analogy. He's so right, that people need different amounts of nurturing and water, and you can't expect immediate results; people develop at different rates and produce at different levels. I've used that process not only in business, but here at the farm as well. I'll show you how I've applied it with the dogs I train for the state police. The process works very well. Of all the people I know, Bill gets the most out of his limited ability."

Everyone laughed as Bill protested, "That's cold. You had me all built up for this great compliment, and then you pulled it right out from under me. Randy, those nice things I said about Nick are all a lie."

Again, the front yard was filled with laughter as the three men began walking toward the patio in the back. The patio had a huge shade tree next to it as well as a rock fountain, making for a relaxing environment. Nick gestured toward the chairs. "You guys grab a seat there and I'll get you both a glass of my homemade lemonade."

"Homemade lemonade . . . Since when have you been in the lemonade business, old buddy?" asked Bill.

"It's something I've been playing around with for the last few months. I think I've got the formula perfected. Just relax and I'll be right back." Nick disappeared through the back door as Randy and Bill chatted about Nick's family background.

Nick returned with three glasses of lemonade; he handed one each to Randy and Bill and set his own down on the table. Randy accepted his glass and took a long drink. "Nick, this lemonade is very good. Don't you think so, Bill?"

Bill finished a long drink of his own and happily replied, "It's excellent."

Nick was happy to see both men enjoying his concoction. Nick looked at Randy and said, "Bill tells me you're progressing very well, but that you may have a few questions for me. How can I help?"

Randy was very happy to have Nick initiate the opportunity to ask questions; he didn't want to seem forward, but he was terribly eager to get some feedback from someone Bill spoke so highly of. "Thanks for taking time out of your day and spending it with me," he told Nick. "You'll never know how much it means to me."

"Not a problem; I hope I can help. I'm no Bill Crocoll, now, but I'll do the best I can," responded Nick. He smiled at them both and took a sip of his lemonade. "Let's take a walk out to the dog kennel while we talk. You can see what I do for fun. When I'm having one of those stressful days, working with the dogs gets my mind off all my problems. Randy, fire away."

As the three men headed toward the dog kennel, Randy started speaking. "I have so many questions for you, I just hope you don't think some of them are stupid." He paused, wondering if he should have brought his notebook.

But before he could continue, Nick interrupted. "Randy, before we get going, let's talk about that. I know some people are hesitant to ask questions, for fear of ridicule. I'm sure some people on your team, perhaps even the person you're having trouble developing, have the same fear, but I learned my lesson about asking dumb questions the first month on my Wall Street job. Do you mind if I share that story with you before you get started with your questions?"

Randy shook his head. "I would love to hear it."

Nick proceeded. "I completed Hubbard and Hahn's orientation and on-boarding program, and then received a phone call from Karl Lis, the divisional vice president, to meet him in his office at ten o'clock. Karl was an MBA from Wharton Business School; the man was simply brilliant. He joined the company after completing his degree at Wharton and quickly rose up within the organization. If you looked up the word 'fast-tracker' in the dictionary, you'd find his picture. It was the quickest rise to the vice president level in the history of the company. He was a class act with clients and potential clients, but he was known throughout the office as an animal. He took no prisoners; when he got a project, it was lights out. He had a very domineering personality and wasn't known for engaging in any personal interactions. He was all business. Have you ever worked with anyone like him?"

Randy thought back to his co-op days and could see a vivid picture of his old boss. "I did work with someone like him, during my co-op at Iowa State. This guy was intense. He was a bulldog when it came to work and with people. He got a lot accomplished, but it was often at the expense the people he worked with. Not too many people liked working with him. The only difference between Karl and him – this guy wasn't that intelligent."

Nick laughed, "It was worse for you, then. At least Karl was super smart. I still remember meeting him for the first time. I was introduced to him on my first day, and he commented that he'd heard I was a hot-shot prospect from GW, but that he'd save his judgment until I had proven myself to him. Really made me feel *very* welcome to the company. Obviously, I was extremely nervous about the meeting. When I arrived at his office, I politely knocked on his door. He waved me in, still working on his computer. There was no 'Hello,' no 'How was orientation?' It was very blunt, and it was my first assignment for the division. Without boring you with the details, the project basically boiled down to me analyzing future market trends in Europe, and the potential impact on the European stock exchange for the next quarter."

Randy interjected, "Your project sounds like something for a more experienced person. No offense, but that assignment sounds awfully high-level for someone's first project."

Nick raised his eyebrows. "Randy, are you saying I wasn't smart enough to handle the assignment?"

Randy felt a lump in his throat. That was the furthest thought from his mind; he knew Nick was very accomplished, and didn't mean to imply otherwise. "Absolutely not! I just, I mean – it sounds really hard. I didn't mean to imply you weren't smart enough."

The People Principles

Nick looked at Bill and both men started laughing. "Randy, I'm just pulling your leg. The project does sound more difficult than it really was. It was basic analytical work, and was actually appropriate for my level. But back to the story. He wanted the project completed by that Thursday, and delivered at the board meeting on Friday with acetates included. We'd meet on Thursday afternoon to review and finalize the presentation, prior to the meeting with the board. I didn't have any questions about the content of the presentation; that part was straightforward. I was very comfortable with analysis, but I didn't have any idea what an acetate was. Rather than asking him, I left the meeting without a clue. I thought that if I asked what seemed to be the simple part of the process, what an acetate was, he'd think I was incompetent. I left the office and got started on the project.

Randy asked, "Before you go any further, what is an acetate? I've never heard of it either."

"I'll get to that in a minute. If I tell you now, it'll ruin the story. So throughout the week, I asked several people what acetates were, but nobody there knew. I finished up the project on Thursday morning, so I called his administrative assistant, Leigh Ellen Thrasher, to ask her what an acetate was; she didn't know either. I told her to tell Karl the presentation was completed and I would see him at three. I went to his office that afternoon thinking that I could finalize the presentation with him, and find out what the heck an acetate was after the meeting. I got to his office and we reviewed the presentation. We made a few minor changes, and then he asked if I had any questions about the meeting or project. I told him no, I was ready for it. As I was getting ready to leave his office he said, 'Oh, one more thing. Leigh Ellen told me that you didn't know what an acetate was – have you found out?' I responded, 'No sir,' but told him I would find out before the meeting the next day. He asked me why I didn't just ask him, and I told him I didn't want to look stupid. I'll never forget his response. He said, 'Well how do you feel right now?' He turned his back and starting working on his computer. I felt like an idiot! From that point forward, I never worried about asking a dumb question."

"Wow, that would've crushed me," Randy said, shaking his head. "So, what is an acetate?"

"An overhead transparency slide. Pretty simple, huh?"

"That's it? An overhead transparency. You went through all that stress over an overhead transparency. Why didn't he just say that, instead of an 'acetate'?" asked Randy.

Nick could appreciate Randy's question; he had wondered the same thing many times. "I never had a chance to ask him. Maybe it was a test to see if I would ask. I'm still not sure why he did it, but boy, was it a valuable lesson for me. Since then, if I have a question about an assignment; or, really, anything, I'm never afraid to ask."

Randy casually kicked a stick that was lying in the grass. He was still pondering why any boss would do such a thing. He looked at Nick and agreed, "Nick, I have to say that is a valuable point. I always feel like I should just know some things, but there are times that I'm honestly clueless when I leave the room after a meeting. Then I scramble to figure out what the person wants, and I waste valuable time in the process. I think I'm getting better about that since I started working with Bill, though. Would you agree, Bill?"

Bill smiled and replied with conviction, "You've come a long way since our first meeting. When we first met, you had your guard up. You were on the defensive. But as you've gained confidence in yourself, and trust in our relationship, it's allowed you to open up your mind to different points of view. You definitely aren't afraid to ask questions, but more importantly, you're open to feedback, and you truly want to grow as a leader."

"I appreciate that. It's been a great learning experience for me. I'm very fortunate to work for such a progressive company, one that truly cares about the development of its people."

The three men arrived at the dog kennel on Nick's farm. Nick reached down to scratch a dog's ear. "These dogs are my pride and joy.

Regardless of how bad a day is going for me, I can always come back here, and like magic, everything's good."

Randy was impressed. The kennels were immaculate, and each dog had his own living area. There were thick trees along the side to give shade during the hot part of the day, and a covered area in each kennel where the dogs could take refuge during inclement weather. "These are beautiful dogs, Nick," Randy said. "I love German Shepherds. I could never have any pets because my younger brother Jeremy was allergic to basically every kind of animal known to man. I love my brother, but I hated those allergies of his. I've always been intrigued by dog training. My Uncle Bib was one of the best hunting dog trainers in our county. People from all over the state would bring their dogs to him to be trained. I got to work with him for a few weeks once, but I imagine training dogs for the state police is pretty different from training dogs to hunt. Can you show me how you do it?"

Nick finished petting the dogs and picked up a few tennis balls to throw for the dogs to chase. He turned toward Randy and replied, "I will, but let me at least answer one of your questions first. I'm dominating the discussion with stories about my life, but we're supposed to be here to discuss yours."

Randy took a quick sip of his lemonade and said, "Oh no, this is extremely interesting, but I will start asking some questions now. Here's my first one. First impressions are so critical in developing relationships; how do you try to connect with people during the first interaction?"

Bill interrupted, "I've heard Nick answer that question many times over the years. He's got a great story, and a technique that really works. I use it all the time."

Nick laughed. "Great, Bill, get Randy all excited about this special approach; he'll have high expectations, and then the big letdown. Nice set-up, bud. It really isn't anything but common sense, but it does work in connecting with others."

Mark J. Balzer

"All right you two," Randy chimed in. "Now you have my curiosity piqued. What's the technique?"

"See, Bill, his curiosity is piqued! Oh well, here goes. I read a story, years ago, about Mary Kay Ash, the cosmetics guru. Her approach with people was simple. She believed that all people go through life with an invisible sign around their neck that says, "Make me feel important." She always tried in all her interactions to make people feel important, especially in the first meeting. Everyone wants to be a somebody, and when someone influences somebody else, it usually influences a lot of bodies. Randy, you look confused. Where'd I lose you?"

One of the dogs came trotting up to Randy, panting eagerly, so Nick handed him a ball and Randy threw it down the hill for the dog to chase. Randy turned towards Nick and smiled slightly. "I'm just trying to process your last statement. Everyone wants to be somebody. I understand that concept. Then did you say someone that influences somebody else, influences a lot of bodies?"

"Remember, you don't influence people one at a time. When you influence someone, you usually influence many more people from that one interaction. I'll explain how that concept works in a few minutes, but are we good to move forward?"

"We're good to go."

"When I meet someone for the first time, I always use this approach, but before I get to that, let me digress for a moment. I'm going to give you a topic you can use with anybody, and they'll stay engaged in the conversation for as long as you keep talking. What do people like to talk about more than anything else?"

Randy shook his head and smiled. "People love to talk about themselves, don't they?"

"Absolutely: we all love to talk about ourselves. Sounds simple, doesn't it? You know what the problem is, Randy?"

The People Principles

"I think so. Instead of letting people tell their story, we all want to tell our own. We want to talk about ourselves. And to be honest, when I meet people, I do it too – I want to tell my story at the expense of theirs. I want to gain their respect, and I do it by telling them about my accomplishments and interests."

Nick replied, "You've got it pegged. We're all guilty of it. But most of us do it for the right reasons; yeah, some people want to brag, but most people just want to impress the other person, gain their approval and establish credibility. The thing we have to remember is that the other person wants to accomplish the same thing when they meet us. We're all self-centered. When you look at a group picture, who do you look for first? And how do you decide whether a picture is good or bad? If you look good in the photo, it's a good picture. If you look bad in the photo, the picture is bad."

Randy and Bill both laughed and Bill chimed in, "Nick, you're absolutely right. If I look good in the picture, it's a good picture." He looked at Randy and added, "You still with us, Randy?"

Randy could easily see what Nick was talking about; he wondered why he hadn't seen this important point himself. He said softly, "I never thought about it before. I've probably used the wrong approach with everyone I've met at Dunkirk. No wonder I haven't connected with some of my team."

Nick looked at Bill and then back at Randy. "Don't be too hard on yourself; most people do the same thing. I did, heck we all did, but if we're telling our life story, do you think we're making the people we meet feel important?"

Randy was trying not to let it get to him, but he knew he'd really dropped the ball on this one. "No, we're too busy trying to make ourselves seem important to them."

Bill added, "Absolutely. We're trying to connect with people, but sometimes we only do it at the intellectual level, by treating them to an infomercial about ourselves. People could care less about your resume – where you graduated from college, or if you even graduated at all. You don't win people over at the intellectual level; you win people over by touching their hearts. If you win their hearts, their minds will follow. The choice is pretty simple. At the end of the conversation with a member of your team, do you want to feel important, or do you want your team member to feel important?"

Randy looked at both men, sensing they knew the answer they were expecting. "I need to make my team feel important, not me. Unfortunately, I'm guilty of making myself feel important most of the time."

Nick chuckled and told him, "Randy, most people do. Not intentionally; they just don't understand what they're really doing. But now you know, and I'm sure the next interaction you have with your team, that person will leave the conversation feeling important. If you want to be an important person, make other people feel important, and you'll become important to them."

"I'll give it my best shot, Nick," replied Randy.

Bill looked at Nick and said, "My friend, do you mind if I give Randy an example?"

Nick shook his head. "I think I know the story you're going to tell. It's one of my favorites. Be my guest."

"Randy, this happened to me during my first year at Dunkirk Distribution, and it's a lesson in leadership I'll never forget. We were having major issues with our inventory control system. Our cycle counts were always off, product was missing or couldn't be found, the customers was furious, the GM was going crazy, and life at the facility wasn't fun. I'd been analyzing the problem for a few weeks and decided to come in over the weekend to examine it in more detail. Casey and I were expecting our first child any day, so you can imagine my wife wasn't happy that I was going in to work on the weekend. Nevertheless, I worked the entire weekend, and thought I'd had a major breakthrough with the inventory problem.

I couldn't wait to get to work on Monday to share the solution with my boss. When I got to work, I rushed to my manager's office and told him what I'd figured out. Before I finish the story, let me ask you a question Randy: when I walked into my manager's office, what do you think I wanted from him?"

Randy thought for a minute. "I'd be looking for a pat on the back – acknowledgment that I'd gone the extra mile, praise for my initiative and effort. Bottom line, I'd want some recognition for my effort. Am I right?"

Both Nick and Bill laughed, and Bill continued with his story. "Yes, I was looking for a 'good job, way to go, we need more people like you' response, but I didn't get it. My boss looked me in the eye and told me I'd wasted a good weekend: my solution had been tried few years back and didn't work then, and it wouldn't work now. He just dismissed my entire idea. Do you know how I felt about him?"

Randy eyes were wide. "I can't believe he did that to you. What a jerk! I'd have been furious. I can only imagine how angry your wife was that you'd been away all weekend, for nothing! I probably would have gotten myself fired; I don't know how I could have kept my mouth shut. What did you do? Did you say something to him?"

Bill grinned, took a sip of his lemonade, and continued his story. "I didn't say a word to him, but I told everyone at the facility about it. I was furious about it at the time, but it was a valuable point for me to learn. I replayed the situation over and over in my head and asked myself, 'What would I have done differently in the situation?' From that point . . . "

Nick interjected, "Bill, before you tell Randy what you did, ask him what he would have done if he were your boss."

"Good call, Nick. So, Randy, how should he have responded to me?"

"Whew." Randy paused to collect his thoughts. "He should have acknowledged your initiative and effort for working on the issue over the weekend. Before he blew off your solution, he should have discussed it with you in detail. Maybe the plan didn't work in the past, but that could have been because the timing was bad, even if the plan was good. You should have walked out of the office feeling good about yourself, not feeling like you did. How's that?"

Nick nodded. "Exactly, we all need confirmation that what we are doing adds value – as you said, a pat on the back. Do you see how Bill's boss influenced him that day?"

"Influenced him?" Randy said, startled. "Bill's boss didn't influence him at all. He sucked all the motivation out of him."

Bill jumped in. "Randy, most people view influence as a good thing, but it can also be negative. Like Nick said, we influence people in every interaction we have with them. We determine through our words and behavior whether the influence is going to be good or bad. Influence doesn't occur in a vacuum. Every time you open your mouth, you influence the person you're talking to. I think you have two options when you speak to another person: you can encourage or discourage them. Either way, influence spreads throughout the team, from person to person, department to department, shift to shift. My not getting validation from my manager had a negative influence on me; then I told everyone I knew about it. So did my manager just influence me, or did he influence others as well?"

"He influenced a lot of people, but in the wrong way," replied Randy.

Nick could see Randy was really soaking this up; he wanted to stress the impact of a positive influence. "Bill and I used to conduct an interpersonal training program together, and our goal was to get through to just one person in the class. If that one person went back and told twenty people about it, how many people had we influenced?"

"You influenced twenty-one people. I get it now: when someone influences somebody else, it usually influences a lot of bodies."

"And if those twenty-one people each influenced twenty-one people, we'd had an influence on forty-two people by our effect on just that one person. Can you see the importance of influence, of making people feel important?"

Randy was actually amazed by the insight he had gained. With a little reservation in his voice he responded, "It's scary how important every interaction is, especially the first one. I'm trying to think of the interactions I had this week and how they went. Did I make people feel important? Probably not."

Nick patted Randy on the back and said, "It's easy to get so caught up in the day-to-day issues that we forget about the people side of leadership. Every interaction we have, we influence others and others influence us. Every interaction is important. I truly believe you win people over in the small moments in life, not the big ones. I'm always amazed by what people remember in an interaction. To you, it may be trivial, but in their life, that small act of kindness, or respect, or sometimes just lending an ear makes a huge difference."

"Randy, how do you feel when someone makes you feel important?" Nick asked.

Randy thought for a brief moment. "It's a great feeling. Working with Bill makes me feel so good about myself, and it shows the commitment the company has made to my development. A few of my friends from college are working at a couple of our competitors, and they've told me some horror stories about their first months. Two of them joined Newman's Distribution Solutions. One started in their facility in Muncie, Indiana, and one in East Aurora, New York. After a daylong orientation program, they were put on third shift without any support. They didn't know the system, didn't know the people, and didn't know anything about leadership. They got the minimum amount of training and had little interaction with their operations manager, and only met their general managers briefly.

Mark J. Balzer

Both of them were frustrated because they have the ability and intelligence to be successful, but they don't have the real life work experience to handle the job. They need what I have here at Dunkirk: a coach and a mentor. It's not just Bill, either. Steve's been down to the floor several times to see me, and the other leaders always have time to answer my questions. People care about me here, and they want me to be successful. I feel bad for my friends that have nobody to turn to. I know they've been sending out their resumes again, after just a month with the company."

"Did you refer them to us?" Bill interjected. "I hate to put my HR hat on, but we're always looking for good people."

Randy laughed and told him, "I didn't need to refer them; they both called me last week and said they'd applied online."

"Fantastic. Sorry about the interruption, Nick; I couldn't control myself."

Nick grinned and threw a few more tennis balls to the dogs. "Not a problem. I'd have been disappointed in you if you didn't. Randy, it's too bad that your friends have had such a negative experience. Everyone needs somebody to take them under their wing. Your friends aren't failing; their company has failed them. I still remember the people that helped me early in my career. Everyone wants and needs that. So I hope I've answered your question, Randy?

Before Randy could respond, Bill told Nick, "You need to tell him about your breakfast with Mary Cook."

Nick knelt down to pet one of his dogs and said, over the dog's delighted rumble, "I think you're right. So I was at a meeting in Chicago, at our Midwest Regional Office. I was leaving my hotel in the morning, not paying attention to much, reading the paper, and I slammed into a lady coming out of her room. I almost knocked her down. I apologized to her immediately, and as she turned around, I realized that the person I'd nearly knocked over was our CEO, Mary

Cook. I couldn't believe it. Of all the people to almost run over, why did it have to be our CEO?

"Mary was a wonderful person. At times you could forget she was the CEO, because she always put you at ease. Anytime you saw her in the hallway or lunchroom, she always took a minute to chat. She didn't play the role of a person in power; she always remembered where she came from. She grew up in a rural community in upstate New York. Her family was very poor, and she had to work to put herself through college, SUNY at Fredonia. Not a household name for finance, but a good college. Got her Master's degree from the University of Buffalo and took some small finance positions with local banks. She was finally hired at O'Connor and Hahn as a junior financial advisor. That's two levels below where I started, but she worked hard, took care of her clients, built her business, and was eventually promoted to a supervisor. She took care of her people; they loved her for it, and it showed in their performance. She moved up quickly in the organization, and she took many people from her team with her as she grew. Like I said, she never forgot where she came from."

Nick paused to take a sip of lemonade. "Sorry for the tangent. After I nearly knocked her down in the hall, I apologized profusely, but she told me not to worry about it. As we both walked toward the elevator, she asked me if I was going to eat breakfast, and I said that I was. What she said next was very small, but extremely powerful. Instead of asking if I would like to join her for breakfast, she asked if *she* could join *me*. Most executives at her level would assume the position of power and say 'Please join me for breakfast.' Not Mary Cook; she really got people.

"After we got our food from the buffet, I started talking about work. She interrupted, though politely, and said, 'Nick, I know what you do for a living, but I don't know anything about your background or family.' She knew what people loved to talk about, and for the next forty-five minutes we discussed my personal history. The thing that I found remarkable was that she was genuinely interested in me. She wasn't doing it for a show, she was engaged in the conversation. I walked away from breakfast on cloud nine. I would do anything for her. I still would today if she called me."

"Randy," Bill jumped in, "Isn't that a great story? Remember, no matter how high you go in the organization, people need to come first. If people come first, the rest of it falls into place. As Nick likes to say, always remember where you came from."

Randy knew they were right. He was also realizing that one aspect of being a leader meant being comfortable and confident enough to give others room to shine. With this in mind he told them, "I agree. I need to stay grounded in who I am and what has made me successful so far. It really is important to give others the same opportunities I've had to feel important and know that they matter."

Nick realized he had talked for a while. "Sorry about the length of my answer; your question must have hit my leadership sweet spot."

Randy wasn't concerned about the time. He was happy and honored to have this valuable and necessary input. "It's been a great discussion, and actually, you've answered several of my questions. Nick, before I ask another one, I have to tell you, I'm amazed at how well-trained your dogs are. I notice that you have them obeying your hand gestures. How long did it take you to train them? How did you do it?"

"To get the dogs to this point in their development takes approximately six weeks. Some are a little faster in their development, while some take a little longer. Just like growing green beans. The process is similar to developing people, too. I start with very small tasks in which I am sure they can be successful. What do you suppose it does for the dog?"

"Hmm . . ." Randy thought for a moment. "It builds their confidence."

"That's the purpose of it. Success builds confidence in animals as well as in people. Every time the dog is successful with a task, I reward it with praise and a milk bone biscuit. If you've ever studied B. F. Skinner, you might remember he taught that behaviors that get rewarded get repeated. Each task gets increasingly more challenging for the dog, but I always make sure the dog is able to perform the task. It's the same with people; they need to be regularly rewarded, with praise if not with a milk bone. Have you ever gone to your manager's office and told him or her to stop praising you?"

Randy shook his head. "Absolutely not. I never get tired of hearing that I'm doing a good job."

Nick chuckled. "Everyone needs it. I need it, Bill needs it, and especially, the person you're developing needs constant encouragement. Give me your most unreliable person, and in one month, I can transform them into one of your most dependable people. I'd start with a task I know the person could complete on time. This would get them going on the right foot, to make them successful and build their confidence. Then I'd give them another task. This task would be a little more complex, but they'd be able to complete it on time, and correctly. Each day I'd give them another task to complete. I'd increase the difficulty of each one, and every time they completed the task, I've give them positive reinforcement. With my feedback and praise, I would get the person to believe they were my go-to person. Randy, have you ever been anyone's go-to person?"

Randy instantly thought of an encouraging experience in college. "Yes, I was a teaching assistant at Iowa State, and I was Doctor Briggs' go-to person."

"And what was the last thing you wanted to do for Doctor Briggs?"

Randy knew the answer instantly. "I never wanted to let Doctor Briggs down."

Nick looked directly at Randy and said, "When you're someone's go-to person, you never want to let that person down. Can you see how you can transform an undependable person into a dependable one? If I can get the undependable person to believe he's my go-to person, the last thing he would want to do would be to let me down."

Randy could see that it was making sense. "I can see how you can do that with people," he agreed. "There isn't anything magical about the process; you just have to be committed to the relationship."

Nick turned to Bill and said, "You should have him watch *My Fair Lady*. It's one of the best examples of the Pygmalion effect that I know of."

Randy interrupted before Bill could respond. "I've watched *The Wizard of Oz* and listened to *Carmen*, but it sounds like I may have to draw the line here. I've never heard of *My Fair Lady*, and I'm sure it's a good old-time movie, but I need something filmed in color, not black and white."

Everyone laughed. "I'll let you off the hook for now," Bill said, "but Nick is right; *My Fair Lady* definitely illustrates the Pygmalion effect. Just think how much culture I can expose you to as I refine your leadership skills."

"Well, Randy," Nick said, "Let me just sum things up before we completely fry your brain. Confidence and success must be followed up with praise and rewards. Every time one of my dogs is successful in completing a task, I give them a milk bone. Think back to Bill's story about when he worked the whole weekend and his manager didn't acknowledge his efforts. When Bill went in to meet with his manager, you said he was looking for a pat on the back. I agree; I'd probably phrase it that he was looking for his milk bone treat. 'Bark, bark, bark, bark, give me my treat!' But instead of getting a treat, Bill got kicked in the mouth. People need to know that their efforts are recognized."

As Nick finished talking, his cell phone rang. He took the call, and then turned back to Randy and Bill and said, "That was my wife. Her car won't start, and she's in town at the mall. Would it be possible to postpone our lunch to another day – or better yet, you could follow me in to the mall, and we can have lunch at the White Village. What do you think?"

Bill looked at Randy. "It's fine with me, so long as I can have a rain check on the burgers you were going to grill. Randy, does that sound good to you?"

"That would be fine. My afternoon is free."

"Great, let's get going. I'll ask my wife to join us, too." Nick gathered the dogs and put them in their kennels. Then the three men walked briskly to the front of the house. They left their empty glasses on the porch, got in their cars, and left for the mall.

Chapter Ten
Twenty Dollar Bill

Randy, Bill, and Nick arrived at the D&F Plaza and found Nick's wife's car in front of Sidey's Department store. She looked relieved to see Nick pull up next to her. They quickly popped the hoods on Nick's and Denise's vehicles and within minutes, the car was started.

Denise blushed and thanked the men for their quick response. "I'm so embarrassed; I feel horrible I broke up your meeting. I was in such a hurry to get to my hair appointment, I left the lights on. I didn't think you were going to bring the cavalry to rescue me, honey, which is even more embarrassing."

"Denise, don't worry about it," Bill said as he gave her a hug. "Two weeks ago I was bringing in groceries and left the key turned in the ignition. The next day my battery was dead, and I had to push the car out to the driveway and have it jumped. It happens to the best of us. Besides, I was hoping to see you anyway. Let me introduce you to Randy Sysol."

Randy shook Denise's hand and said, "It's very nice to meet you, Ma'am. Thank you for sharing your husband with me today."

"Ma'am? I like you already! You must not be from around here. That's very sweet of you; Nick was like that when we first met, but please call me Denise."

Nick said to Denise, "Honey, I'm going to take the car around the block a few times to charge up the battery; do you mind giving Bill and Randy a tour of 'world famous' Sidey's for a few minutes?"

"No problem at all," Denise replied.

Randy had wanted to write things down all morning but hadn't had his notebook with him. "Actually, Nick," he said, "that would be perfect. I've been learning a lot this morning, but I didn't bring a notebook. We could run into Sidey's and get one."

Denise nodded. "I think they have pretty good selection of smaller notebooks that you can carry with you anywhere. Let's go have a look."

"By the way," Nick told Denise, "I'm still that sweet young man you fell in love with, and to prove it, I'd like you to join us for lunch when I get back. We're going to the White Village."

Denise smiled at Nick. "I appreciate the invitation, but I'm sure you guys want to finish your meeting. I've interrupted you enough already."

Before Nick could respond, Bill jumped in. "Denise, I think I speak for Randy as well as myself: we would be hurt if you didn't join us. I haven't seen you since Nick's surprise birthday party in February, which was two months ago. Besides, Nick and I have nothing left to teach Randy; our knowledge is tapped out."

Denise shook her head. "I don't believe that for one second, Mr. Crocoll; you have more good leadership stories than any one person should have. But if you're sure I'm not interrupting your meeting, I'd love to join you. Really, how can I pass it up? I don't remember the last time I was escorted to lunch by three handsome men."

Nick replied, "Then it's settled. I'll be back in a few and then we'll head over to the White Village."

Nick drove off, and the rest of the crew went in to Sidey's to get a notebook for Randy. About ten minutes later, Nick called Denise and let her know he was outside looking for a parking place. They went out to wait for him.

Randy was examining his notebook when Nick arrived. Nick asked, "Well, Randy, did you find something that will work?"

Randy laughed and replied, "With everything I'm learning today, I'm not sure it has enough pages . . ."

Everyone laughed as they walked to the restaurant, in the plaza next to Sidey's. They were seated in the front of the restaurant, overlooking a beautiful water fountain built in 1976 for the bi-centennial celebration. "Denise, how is everything going at work?" asked Bill.

"Great. We've been working with Hutchinson Electronics on a teambuilding project and we just finished the initial training session of the Essentials of Leadership II. The folks at Hutchinson are great, and they're really embracing our approach. I love working with people that are committed to building a better company. Matt Hutchinson gets it in a big way. Our next step will be a workshop on developing their team values, mission and vision statements, and goals and objectives to meet their four-year strategic business plan."

Randy's eyes opened wide. "Excuse me, Denise, are you involved in leadership and development training, too?"

Denise smiled and replied, "Oh, I'm sorry, Randy. I assumed Nick had told you that. I guess he was so busy passing on his wisdom to you that my darling husband forgot to mention what I do." She paused to give Nick a sly look that made everyone at the table laugh. Turning back to Randy, she continued, "I'm in training and development. I own a consulting firm that specializes in leadership development and career coaching. Our company is called The Leadership Circle. We're not very big – a total of fifteen employees and five steady clients – but over the course of any given year we do work with thirty-five to forty companies."

"Doesn't sound small to me," responded Randy

"Thank you. There are a few consulting companies in the Dunkirk-

The People Principles

Fredonia area that are part of nationwide firms with hundreds of clients, but we hold our own. Their wrapper is fancier than ours, but I think we have better substance. We pride ourselves on the quality of our programs and solutions." Before Randy could respond, the waitress came to the table to take their drink orders.

After the waitress had gone, Randy asked, "Ma'am, do you mind if I ask you a few questions?"

"There you go with that ma'am stuff again."

Randy looked somewhat embarrassed. "Sorry, Denise. Can I ask you a few questions about your firm and experiences as a business consultant?"

"That's much better. Bill and Nick may have a problem with it, but I sure don't mind." Denise turned to Nick and Bill. "Do you fellows mind if I answer a few questions for Randy?"

"Not at all. She actually knows more than both of us," responded Bill.

"Bill, you always know the right thing to say," laughed Denise.

Randy began, "My first question is about vision. How do I explain the importance of vision to my team?"

Denise looked surprised. "You don't mess around with small-time leadership questions; you want to get right to the important ones. I'm impressed that at your age, you recognize the need for a vision. I've worked with CEOs that don't understand the importance of a vision. Bill, where did you find him?"

Before Bill could answer, Randy interjected, "Are you serious? There are CEOs that don't believe in having a mission and vision statement for their company? Giving people a vision is Leadership 101. I don't want to sound like a know-it-all, but I do know that much about leadership."

Denise smiled at Randy as the waitress returned to the table with their drinks. Everyone quickly looked over the menu and ordered. Randy went with the lunch special; meatloaf and mashed potatoes reminded him of his mom's cooking. Denise, Bill, and Nick all ordered the cream and chicken soup with a salad.

After the waitress left, Denise continued, "There are more of them than I care to mention. Their entire focus is the bottom line. Words like 'mission' and 'vision' aren't in their vocabulary, and heaven forbid you suggest they try to develop a high-performing culture. They almost come out of their skin; it's like preaching Communism to them." Denise took a sip of water. "They don't understand how much more profitable their company would be if they had a mission and vision in place. They leave so much money on the table it's unbelievable. These people are highly educated; many of them are from the best colleges in the country. I just cannot . . ."

Before she could finish her sentence, Nick interrupted her. "Denise, honey, you're up on your soapbox again. I know your passion for mission and vision, but I'm sure Randy has more than one question for you."

Denise smiled, closed her eyes, and took a deep breath. "You're right. I'm sorry, Randy. As you can see, I'm a huge believer in vision. Show me a company or team without a vision, I'll show you a complacent organization. Vision creates excitement!"

Randy smiled. "Don't worry about it. Your passion is contagious. You've got me fired up about the importance of mission and vision. I love it! How come some CEOs don't get it?"

"That's an excellent question, Randy. One point of clarification, though: it's not just CEOs that don't get the importance of a vision. In my experience, three-quarters of leaders don't understand its importance."

Randy nodded his head. "That's incredible. I believe it, but it's so hard for me to get my head around. Why is it so difficult for leaders to understand that teams need direction?"

Denise smiled at Randy. "One reason is that many companies hire a business consultant to create their vision for them. Of course the consultant uses all the buzzwords. You know the ones: 'world-class,' 'quality-oriented,' 'excellent customer service,' 'innovative,' etc. When people read the vision it doesn't have any meaning for them. It reads 'blah, blah, customer service, blah, blah quality-oriented.' Most companies' mission and vision statements sound the same. They don't get people excited about the future of *their* company. Leaders can check it off their to-do list, but it sounds like a Charlie Brown conversation to the employees."

Everyone at the table laughed. "Denise, I really miss your perspective on business. It's refreshing," said Bill.

Nick chimed in, "But don't you think trying to explain the importance of vision is very difficult because most people see vision as something abstract, rather than real?"

Denise smiled at her husband. "Now you're baiting me. You know that question will get me back on my soapbox."

"I know it will, honey, but I think it's important for Randy to get a complete picture of the importance of a vision."

Denise looked at Randy and asked, "Randy, do you mind if I get a little preachy?"

"I want to hear it all. Don't worry about Bill and Nick. Believe me, they've been on their own soapboxes a few times."

"Very good, then; as Paul Harvey would say, 'Here is the rest of the story.'" Everyone laughed out loud as Denise took another sip of her water. Just as she was getting ready to continue, the waitress brought their food to the table. They thanked her and told her the food looked great. After she'd walked away, Denise continued, "A good vision is real, and you can see and feel it. It's not abstract if it's done right. When you walk into a building, you can feel it in the air, and you can see it the faces and voices of the people that work there. It's alive! Here's the key: you have to make people feel the vision. Words alone don't do justice. When you communicate a vision, the words need to come from a leader's heart, not from their lips."

Randy interrupted her, "I love that last statement. The words must come from a leader's heart, not their lips. That's powerful. I need to learn to speak like those leaders." He reached for his notebook and started writing.

Denise waited for Randy to finish writing, and then started with a word of encouragement. "You already do that, Randy; your passion is visible to me. You'll make your vision come alive and people will accept it and feel it in their hearts. Once you get people to feel something, they usually buy into it, and once they have bought into the idea, the creation and implementation of the mission and vision go smoothly. I think that covers that question."

The waitress stopped by to make sure everyone's meals were just right and to check on refills. Everyone assured her that everything was perfect. When she had gone, Randy continued, "One last question about mission and vision before we leave the topic. I know you said you need to speak from your heart and not from your lips. Are there any other ways to make people really feel an abstract topic?" asked Randy.

Both Bill and Nick looked at Denise, anticipating her response. Denise said, "I'd do the following exercise with your team. Get enough blindfolds for half of your team, some duct tape, and eight to ten bandanas." Randy wrote those items in his notebook as Denise spoke. "Tape off a twelve foot by twelve foot square with the duct tape, and lay the bandanas throughout the square. Make sense so far?"

Randy was writing again. "Yes," he responded.

"At your next meeting, announce to the team that they'll be doing

The People Principles

a teambuilding exercise. Divide them up into pairs and give them the following instructions: You and your partner will be required to cross a minefield. The bandanas are the mines. One member of the partnership will be blindfolded and will count on the other person for directions. The person without the blindfold must safely direct their partner across the minefield without stepping on a mine. They'll have three minutes to cross the square."

Randy was writing everything down, so Denise took a bite of her salad and patiently waited. When he looked up, she continued, "Once they've crossed the square, the other person will be blindfolded and will have to cross it the other way. Take your team to the minefield and line them up across from each other on the square. Blindfold one side of the team and tell the people that on the count of three, the exercise will begin and all teams will go at once."

Randy looked up from his notebook, a bit confused. "Did you say everyone goes at once?"

"Yes, everyone begins at once," responded Denise.

"Wow, it must be total chaos." Randy shook his head. "I have thirty people on my team. How can they hear their partner's direction if everyone's yelling at the same time?"

Denise grinned. "That's the point of the exercise. It's almost impossible to distinguish your partner's voice from someone else's partner, and a lot of people will get blown up in the process. When you discuss the exercise with them after the two rounds, not being able to hear or distinguish their partners voice will be one of the biggest complaints they have. They'll tell you they were counting on their partner for directions, but couldn't hear them and didn't know what voice to listen too. So, Randy, in this exercise, what does each blindfolded player need from their partner?"

Randy swallowed a bite of meatloaf and thought for a moment. "Well, they need to trust their partner. Their partner can act as their eyes and they count on them for direction. The problem is that there are too many people giving different directions."

"Very good assessment, Randy. This exercise is typical of many organizations I work with. They don't have a vision, the leadership team isn't on the same page, employees are confused and frustrated because they're getting mixed messages from the leadership team, other employees are giving them their spin on the operation, and it's just a bunch of noise without a clear direction. This manager says one thing, while another manager says another, and they get different information from their peers, too. Who should the employees listen too? Who should they trust? Does it sound like the exercise?"

"It's exactly like the exercise: total chaos."

"And why is it total chaos?" asked Denise.

"There's no clear direction. There's no singular voice, and no clear communication. Everyone's taking a different path through the minefield," responded Randy.

"Now, tie the exercise back to the workplace. Ask them how they felt during the exercise? What would have helped them through the minefield? They'll make your point for you about the importance of having a team vision. You won't need to sell the rationale for your vision, they'll sell it to you, and more importantly, they'll sell it to themselves. You'll have made them feel the need for a vision."

Randy's mind was racing; he could see how the whole group would be caught up in the excitement of the exercise, and how this exercise would help make the need for a team vision so clear. "It's amazing how you make a topic come alive and people feel the concept. This would be a great exercise for the team, and you're okay with me using it, right?"

"Absolutely! If it will help, please do."

The People Principles

"Thank you; I'm really looking forward to trying it out. Are you ready for my next question?"

Denise smiled. "I don't want your meatloaf to get any colder than it may already be; besides, Nick and Bill are just about done with their meals. But when we're done, would you indulge me for just a few more minutes? I'd like to elaborate a little more on our discussion."

Randy nodded and raised his hand slightly. "When I finish my meatloaf, I'm all ears. Bill and I spoke about mission and vision last week and I'd like any additional insight you can provide." Denise and Randy started eating.

After they'd all finished their meal and chatted idly for a few minutes, Denise looked at Randy and said, "May I start with some of my additional thoughts?"

Randy replied, "Absolutely."

Denise smiled. "You are eager to learn. Okay, the vision has to be a shared vision, it can't just be yours. Get people involved in developing the vision. Give them ownership. At first you'll find that having the entire team's input is overwhelming and tedious. You'll need to 'wordsmith' what they give you to finalize the vision. It might seem difficult, but developing the vision is actually the easy part. Making the vision come alive, though, is tough. Most visions fail because leaders don't live it. You have to see it, believe it, and be it." Randy motioned his hand to stop Denise before she made her next point. "Do you have a question?"

"What do you mean, 'see it, believe it, and be it'?"

Nick glanced at Bill, smiling. "Put your seat belt on, buddy. This is going to get good now. I love this explanation."

Denise gave Nick a smirk and said, "Don't listen to him. He always tells people that, but so far, I've never had anyone actually fall out of their chair."

Nick interjected, "You almost lost me when you had this discussion with my last manager. Remember that conversation?"

Denise replied in a serious voice, "He deserved every word I said; don't even get me started on that man. He was living in the Stone Age, but we can tell that story later. Where was I?" She paused to collect her thoughts. "Oh, yes. Randy, you need to be able to see your vision, crystal clear, in your mind. You have to see it in bright colors, every detail of what it will look like when it's completed and successful. It has to be vivid. An image is more powerful than an idea, because the mind cannot separate image from reality. Are you still with me?"

"I am, just give me a minute to write that down." Randy quickly wrote down Denise's last point about images and looked up. "Okay. I'm all caught up, and all ears."

"Next you have to believe it from the top of your head to the tips of your toes. You can't have any doubts. Please hear me loud and clear on this point. You cannot have *any* doubts." Denise stopped speaking to let her words sink in. "If you have doubts, you'll retreat at the first sign of trouble or conflict. I've seen it so many times with leaders; they hit their first barrier, and they back off to hide in their safe place. It takes courage to implement a vision, and many leaders lack the intestinal fortitude to see it to the end. Are you are drinking the Kool-Aid yet, Randy?"

Randy's facial expression showed he was fully engaged with Denise's message, and he responded, "Oh, I'm drinking the Kool-Aid. This is good stuff. Implementing a vision is pretty intense! You have to have some pretty strong will power, don't you, Denise?" Randy started writing again, and the waitress came by to gather up the empty plates and offer dessert. Everyone smiled and declined.

Denise thought for a moment about Randy's comment. Then she looked straight at him and said in a low, serious tone, "Will power isn't enough. You need *want* power. You have to want it so bad that nothing is going to prevent you from accomplishing your dream.

The People Principles

Want power, not will power. Trust me; will power won't see you through those difficult times when people start doubting the vision. This is when you have to reach deep down inside of yourself and have the belief in the vision. Will power can let you drift into self-doubt; want power keeps you strong and moving forward. Do you see the difference?"

The table was silent as everyone waited for Randy's answer. "Yes, I do. I can definitely see why you need want power over will power. Actually, I've never heard of want power, but I know what it is now!" Everyone laughed out loud. Randy started writing again; when he finished, he asked, "Are you going to explain how leaders make the vision come alive?"

The other three all chuckled. Denise said, "I need to get to that, sorry. The reason many visions fail is because leaders make a plaque of the vision, place it on the wall, and think they're done. They're short-sighted. How's that going to create excitement in their business? Creating and making a vision isn't a twelve-step program, nor is it an item on your to-do list. A vision is a process, to create a better future for your team and your organization. You become the vision, based upon your daily behavior."

Randy was listening intently, but he was a little lost. "Let me interrupt you. How do you become the vision through your behavior?" Denise smiled. "Did I say something funny?" asked Randy in response to Denise's smile.

She assured him, "Absolutely not. Bill told me you were driven and very inquisitive. I love your desire to learn. Let me answer your question. You have to be the communicator, the enforcer, the gatekeeper; you have to be the vision. That's the last part of 'see it, believe, and be it.' People should be able to see the vision in all that you do. This is where courage comes into the picture. You have to have courage to see it through. Most leaders abandon their vision at the first sign of trouble. Many leaders – or rather managers – lack the courage to overcome obstacles. They're tree huggers, afraid to go out on a limb. What they don't realize is that all the fruit is at the end of the branches. Randy, go pick the fruit. If the branch breaks, so what? Dust yourself off and climb back up the tree. Go pick the fruit at the end of the branches. We all fall down in life. Success is getting up one more time than you've been knocked down."

Randy interjected, "I like your definition of success. I won't stay down on the ground and feel sorry for myself. I'm not a quitter. I'll get back up and climb the tree again. My mother always told me, whatever doesn't kill you will make you stronger. And I've had plenty of opportunities to get stronger in my life," Randy chuckled and said again, "Believe me, plenty of opportunities."

Denise nodded in approval. "I love your attitude. It shows me that you have the courage to be a visionary leader. Think of the courage Christopher Columbus needed to accomplish his vision. Columbus was telling anyone in Europe who would listen to him that he could sail to the East Indies. I'm sure he was mocked, ridiculed, and called crazy. But that didn't stop him. His conviction was supported by his unwavering courage. If you study successful people, most of them, like Columbus, had to overcome some type of adversity to achieve success. Columbus kept communicating his vision, and he finally convinced Queen Isabella and King Ferdinand to finance his journey. Next, he had to sell his vision to others, and he finally convinced forty-one men to help him accomplish his vision. That couldn't have been easy. After being at sea for thirty days without seeing land, some of his crew began to mutiny against him. This didn't make him turn around, because he never lost sight of his vision, and he eventually found a new world. Now that took courage. Most managers lack this kind of courage. They do don't have a personal constitution or moral conviction of right and wrong."

Bill jumped into the conversation and said, "Before Randy asks you another question, how come you never shared that point about Columbus with me, Denise? It's great; I can use it in my teambuilding class."

"Simple; you never asked," answered Denise with a sly grin.

The entire table broke out in laughter. "Fair enough! Randy, don't you have another question for her?" Bill said wryly.

"Okay, here goes: what are the keys to developing others?" asked Randy.

"Another good question. I think Bill and Nick may have a different answer for that one, but I think we all have a common thread when it comes to people. When you discuss leadership, it's all about the people. People are the alpha and omega in any leadership discussion. The major key is getting people to believe in themselves. Most people fail to reach their potential, not from lack of skills and ability, but from a poor self-concept. People need to like themselves." Denise thought for a moment. "No, people need to love themselves. I don't mean people need to stand in front of a mirror and say 'This is the prettiest picture in the whole house,' but people need to love themselves. Ask yourself: if you don't love yourself, then who will? I often ask people in class what they like about themselves, and ninety percent of them don't have a clue. People know why they like other people. But when it comes to understanding themselves, they've never thought through what they like about the person they are."

Randy held his hand up and said, "Denise, this seems important. Give me just a moment to write it down."

Nick chuckled and said, "Would you like me to go next door and get you another notebook, Randy?"

Bill chimed in, "You may need to get him another pen as well."

Both men laughed; Randy rolled his eyes and kept writing.

When he stopped writing, Denise continued without missing a beat. "It's really a simple question. You ask a person to name someone they admire, and to tell you what they admire about them. They'll list fifteen or twenty characteristics that they like about that individual. Then ask that same person what they like about themselves, and they'll struggle to come up with three things. It always amazes me that they don't know what they like about themselves. But that's because they're constantly beating themselves up – over seventy-five percent of self-talk is negative. What do think, Randy?"

Before Randy could answer, Nick interjected. "Did you hear that, Bill? Stop looking at yourself in the mirror and telling Casey your house needs more of them."

Bill had just taken a big swallow of his drink so he couldn't respond, except to close his eyes and shake his head.

Denise smirked at Nick. "Randy, don't mind my husband; he thinks he's a part-time comedian. You look like you're not really buying into the concept of loving yourself."

Randy thought for a moment before he responded. "Well, to be honest, I'd struggle to tell you what I like about myself." He paused to see Denise's reaction, but she looked impassive, waiting for the answer to her question. "*Love* is such a strong word; I'm more comfortable with the 'liking yourself' concept, I guess."

Denise looked down at the table and fidgeted with her straw. "I know 'love' is a strong, emotional word, and it's not often used in the business world. People are uncomfortable with the concept of loving yourself –it sounds so arrogant and self-centered. But I see a parallel between the concept of liking yourself and loving yourself, and the difference between 'will power' and 'want power'. Liking yourself is a good start, but liking isn't deep enough for me."

Randy set his pen on the table and rubbed his chin. "I guess I see your point, but I'm still having a hard time getting my head around it. I just don't think about myself in that way. I'll need to give that one some thought. Sorry."

Denise could see that Randy was really trying to process this new way of thinking. She replied warmly, "Randy, don't apologize for the way you think. We're all entitled to our beliefs. We can just agree to disagree, for the moment. But you do have to give some thought to what you like about yourself. If you don't like yourself, who will?"

Nick interjected, "Hey, that's not fair – you've never let me off the hook with 'we'll just to agree to disagree.' Why does Randy get special treatment, Denise?"

"Let me handle this one," Bill chuckled. "See, Randy makes some valid points, while your arguments usually lack validity. Your thinking has to be corrected for your own sake." Everyone at the table laughed except Nick. "Come on, now, I had to get you back for that line about me and mirrors."

Denise folded her arms, leaned back into her chair, and shook her head slowly from side to side. Then she looked at Nick and Bill and said, "All right, you two, can you keep your commentary to yourselves? Randy and I are trying to have an intelligent conversation over here."

Nick glared at Bill and said, "Great Bill, now you got me in trouble."

Denise laughed. "Don't mind those two characters, Randy. Where were we?"

Randy answered hesitantly, "We were agreeing to disagree on the 'like yourself' versus 'love yourself' concepts."

Denise said, "That's right; let's discuss self-concept for a minute. Do you believe you can impact a person's sense of self-worth through your behavior as a leader?"

"I do believe we can impact a person's self-worth with our behavior, but I need to add a qualifier."

"A qualifier? Why do you need to add a qualifier? I agree with your statement without one."

"We can only impact a person's self worth if they lack confidence,"

Randy explained. "If a person has confidence in themselves, I don't believe another person's behavior or comments can hurt their self worth. Strong people don't allow others to make them feel anything they don't want to feel. I'm not going to allow another person's perception of me to diminish my confidence. I don't need another person's approval to feel good about who I am. I'm perfectly confident in my ability to get the job done." Randy sat back in his chair to let Denise digest his explanation.

"Interesting point. I never looked at it from that perspective before. Let me noodle on that for a minute." Denise sat back in the chair as the table became strangely quiet. Randy began to fidget in his chair while Bill and Nick looked away from him. "Strong people are immune from negative comments. Hmmm . . . So what determines whether a person has confidence in themselves or not, Randy?"

The waitress returned to ask if there would be anything else. Everyone told her no, thank you, and as she cleared the remaining plates, Randy began to answer Denise's question. Nick and Bill grinned down at the table as she told Denise, "A lot of things determine a person's confidence. Their past successes, accomplishments, abilities, education, and . . ."

Randy began to smile back at Nick and Bill. Denise asked, "And what, Randy? Did you lose your train of thought?"

"And if a person believes in their ability, and likes who they are."

Denise couldn't resist pushing the issue further. "And the more a person likes themselves, perhaps even loves themselves, the more self-confidence and self-worth they'll have?"

Randy began to shakes his head. "You guys are masters at setting me up to make me eat my words. Man, I hate when that happens. Bill does it to me all the time." Randy knew he was caving. "Yes, the more a person likes themselves, the more self-confidence the person will have, but I can't concede the love part yet."

Denise laughed and said, "That's fine, Randy; at least you're open to exploring the idea. I do believe that, as you reflect on the concept, you'll eventually accept the importance of loving yourself. Let's get back to the way leadership behavior impacts the self-concept of people on the team.

"As leaders, we play a very important part in determining people's self-worth. We can build people up or tear them down with our words and actions. And once a person buys into a perception of him or herself, it's really difficult to change. I had a friend who was removed from the college prep program in high school by her guidance counselor. He basically told her to focus on business-related classes and prepare her for a career as an administrative assistant. She bought into his perception of her, and she tailored her curriculum to match his perception of her ability. She didn't think she was smart enough to get a four-year degree. She attended a two-year business college, but never graduated. She took some low-level clerical jobs while her fiancé finished his degree, and eventually earned a PhD in psychology. He was part of a research team on IQ and gave his wife an IQ test. When they scored the assessment, her IQ was actually greater than his. For thirty-five years of her life she didn't think she was smart, when in reality, she was a genius. She bought into the perception other people had of her. She had low self-esteem. Today she has her PhD as well, and she heads up an engineering department with a hi-tech company in Germantown, Maryland – this same person whose high school guidance counselor told her she didn't have the intellect to attend college. Once she changed her perception of herself, it opened up a whole new world of opportunities. She was always brilliant, but she didn't view herself that way. It's amazing what people can accomplish if they believe in themselves."

As Randy reacted to Denise's story, the waitress brought the check and Nick pulled a wad of crumpled-up twenty-dollar bills from his pocket.

Randy said, "What a remarkable story. It's a little unbelievable. Was she mad at that guidance counselor?"

Denise reached towards Nick and said, "Honey, would you give me one of those twenty dollar bills?" She turned back to Randy. "Before I answer your question, let me ask you a few questions first. I saw this at a seminar I attended last year. Look at this crumpled-up twenty-dollar bill. Would you want it?"

Randy immediately replied, "Sure, if you were giving it to me."

Denise stood up from the table and crushed the twenty dollar bill into a ball, threw it on the floor, and rubbed it into the carpet with her shoe. "Now would you want this twenty dollar bill?"

"Absolutely, why wouldn't I want it?"

"Why *would* you want it?" shot back Denise.

Randy replied without hesitating, "Whatever you do to it, it keeps its value. It's still worth twenty dollars."

"Exactly, and people are like twenty dollar bills. We come out of the womb clean and crisp, but there are times in life when we get crumpled and dropped, times when we get stepped on. The thing we need to remember is that, despite all of those things, people retain their value. You should never let someone else determine what you're worth. You determine it yourself. So to answer your question, is she mad at her guidance counselor? Absolutely not; she's mad at herself. She let someone else decide her value as a person, and she knows you have to take one hundred percent responsibility for yourself. Too many people play the blame game: it's always someone else's fault, never their own. I don't play that game anymore. I control my destiny, period."

Randy knew exactly what Denise was saying. People were valuable, and regardless of any past issues, they retained their value. It was disturbing that someone in an authority position would use their influence so destructively. He thought back to a negative experience with a previous manager, and decided to share it with Denise.

"That's a powerful story, Denise. I remember in the past, I had one manager that I just couldn't make happy. He was always on me about something, and he told me I wouldn't amount to anything unless I changed my ways. I tried everything to win him over. All I wanted was to hear him say, 'Randy, you're doing a good job, and you have what it takes to make it.' He never said it, not one time, and it haunted me for the longest time. I still think about it from time to time."

Nick and Bill both nodded thoughtfully, knowing exactly the situation he was describing; they had seen it happen numerous times.

Denise leaned forward in her chair, rested her arms on the table, and said, looking intently at Randy, "I've seen that kind of thing over and over again. Why was pleasing him so important to you? You were a still a good person, with or without his approval. What made his opinion matter?"

Randy knew she was right; his value didn't depend on another person's opinion. He thought a moment and then replied, "It really shouldn't. It really depends on what criteria we use to evaluate ourselves; was the problem with my manager and his lack of effective leadership skills, or was it my responsibility to discover my own value?" He smiled. "Denise, you hit it right on. I was still a good person, whether he thought so or not. I didn't need his approval to know my value as a person. People are like twenty- dollar bills. You can beat them up, stomp on them, or knock them down, but the only person's opinion that counts in the end is the individual's. Thank you so much for sharing this story with me. It's given me a sense of freedom from my past, and reminds me that I need to be a positive influence as a leader."

Denise was encouraged to hear that Randy understood the importance of her story. She assured him, "Always remember, anyone's opinion of you is only one person's opinion. Appreciate their feedback, but don't let one person's opinion determine who you are and wreak havoc on your sense of self-worth. I think all people question their value as a person from time to time. I was one of the worst. I had zero confidence in myself and I looked to others to build me up. I needed their approval and affirmation. When I didn't get it, I was a train wreck. I hated that weakness in myself. "

Randy was shocked. "I can't believe you ever doubted yourself. You come across so confident and self- assured. You're the last person I would ever think had a problem with self-esteem. Seriously, it's hard to believe." He paused and looked around the table and then back to Denise. "Are you setting me up for another learning point?"

Nick and Bill laughed; Denise leaned back into her chair and laughed as well. "No, it's not a set-up," she said, "but seriously, believe it. I was one of the worst. One bad comment from someone would send me into a tailspin. It could be the smallest thing and I was crushed. I depended so much on what other people said about me. I didn't want it to be that way, but unfortunately, I'd developed a pattern of giving others the power to determine my worth."

Randy could see the disappointment in Denise's face. "I believe you, but it's still hard to imagine you suffering from a poor self-concept. No one would be able to tell you had self-esteem issues by talking to you today." Randy paused for a moment and then asked, "If you don't mind me asking, what turned you around?"

Denise turned her gaze toward Nick and pointed at him. "It was when I started dating him. I thought, if someone that good-looking could be attracted to me, I must have something going for me." Nick was sipping his coffee and began to choke. "You okay, honey?" Denise asked.

Nick's eyes were wide. "You never told me that. You almost killed me right there. So it was my good looks that turned you round that corner? Bill, I hope you're listening to this. It was my good looks that got Denise to where she is today."

Denise grinned at Nick and told him, "No, it wasn't your good looks; I just wanted to see if you were still paying attention. Talk about an ego."

Bill chimed in, "Yes, Nick, I'm listening to the entire conversation. So it wasn't Nick's good looks that did it. I couldn't imagine his looks could turn you around. Turn you off, yes, but turn you around, no."

Everyone laughed, including Nick, who replied, "Denise, I believe you were telling Randy what turned your self-image around. Can we get back to the explanation, please? My self- concept is starting to wither." As Nick finished talking, Bill's cell phone rang and he excused himself from the table.

"Sure thing, honey, Sorry for doing that to you. In all honesty, Nick was a huge part of my transition. He's one of the most amazing people I know, and I'm so fortunate to have him in my life."

"Thanks, Denise. I feel the same way about you. May I ask one favor?"

"Sure thing, what would you like?"

"Can you repeat what you just said when Bill comes back?"

Randy looked at Nick and Denise and laughed. "You guys are too much. I love the fun you have with each other. You guys are a blast!" he said.

Denise replied, "Thank you, Randy. We do have a great relationship, built on the concepts we teach to others. We truly practice what we preach." She realized they had wandered from the original question Randy had asked, and she had forgotten her point. "I'm sorry, Randy. What was your question again?"

Randy had to think for a second as well. "How did you gain confidence in yourself, other than through Nick's good looks?"

Both Nick and Denise smiled as Bill returned to the table. Nick asked, "Everything cool?"

Bill replied, "Yeah, everything's cool."

Denise answered Randy's question with a bit of a grin. "I know this is going to sound corny, but a Whitney Houston song. 'The Greatest Love of All.' It was my starting point. Are you familiar with the song?"

Randy looked around the table before he responded, hoping someone might help him out. "She's a little before my time, and I'm more of a heavy metal guy. I do enjoy other types of music, but I don't know that song."

"Did you say 'before your time?'" Before Randy could answer, Denise laughed and explained, "Just to set the record straight, she's still alive and performing. I keep the words to a portion of the song in my purse, and if self-doubt starts creeping into my psyche, I read them. They help me refocus on what I love about myself."

"Can I see them, please?" asked Randy.

"Absolutely." Denise reached into her purse and handed Randy a laminated piece of paper. "If you don't mind, read it out loud."

"Sure thing." Randy began reading the words out loud from the paper Denise had handed him.

> *Everybody is searching for a hero*
> *People need someone to look up to*
> *I never found anyone who fulfills my needs*
> *A lonely place to be*
> *So I learned to depend on me*
> *I decided long ago, never to walk in anyone's shadow*
> *If I fail, if I succeed*
> *At least I'll live as I believe*
> *No matter what they take from me*
> *They can't take away my dignity*
> *Because the greatest love of all*
> *Is happening to me*
> *I found the greatest love of all*
> *Inside of me*

*The greatest love of all
Is easy to achieve
Learning to love yourself
It is the greatest love of all*

When Randy had finished reading the lyrics, the table fell silent as everyone reflected on the words. Finally Denise spoke up. "I know the song may sound a little sappy, but it hits home with me. Many times, they've helped me channel my thoughts in the right direction when I was down or stressed out. Randy, do you have any thoughts or feedback? Your lack of response is unusual."

"Sorry about that, I was thinking over the lyrics here, and how they apply to me. I can see how they could help you out if you start doubting yourself. The more you illustrate this 'love yourself' concept, the more I'm coming around. I'm getting there, slowly."

"Randy, I didn't share those lyrics with you to hammer home the concept of loving yourself." Randy tried to interrupt, but Denise raised her hand to prevent him from breaking into her explanation. "You asked me how I improved my self-concept, and listening to that song opened my eyes. There were many other factors involved in improving my self-worth, but those words gave me a new perspective and started the process. They were powerful then, and they're powerful now."

Randy's face had turned slightly red. "Denise, I'm sorry if my comment offended you. The words to the song are powerful, and I can see how important they are to you – and they've obviously helped you. I was just thinking out loud, and the words didn't come out exactly the way I meant for them to."

"Randy, no offense taken. Those words are my compass when I start going the wrong way. They help ground me in positive self-talk."

Nick interjected, "I hate to interrupt, but our waitress has been looking in our direction quite a bit. I think she wants our table for the people lined up outside. We can continue the conversation at our house, if you want."

Everyone got up from the table. Bill added an extra twenty percent to the tip to make up for the time they had taken at the table, and they walked out through the crowded lobby. Once they had reached the cars, Bill asked Randy if he'd like to continue the conversation at Nick's house.

Randy answered, "Thanks, Bill, but I think I've taken up enough of everyone's time, and I really need to get back to my house. I have a few friends coming over tonight. Nick and Denise, I just want to thank you both for spending time with me today. It was invaluable. Like a MasterCard commercial: priceless."

Denise handed Randy her business card and said, "You're more than welcome, and if you need any help, please give me a call."

Nick added, "Remember, if we can help you in any way, just let us know. I enjoyed the afternoon, and I think you're going to do great at Dunkirk Distribution. If I were Bill, I'd be updating my resume." Everyone looked at Bill and laughed. The four of them said their goodbyes, headed to their cars, and drove away.

As Bill and Randy headed back to Bill's place, Randy started writing in his notebook. Bill wanted to give Randy some time to himself so he could review the day, which had been packed with new and interesting principles. He reached over and turned on the radio, turning to his favorite eighties music station. He glanced over and saw Randy tapping his pen to the beat of the music.

As they got closer, Randy stopped writing and looked over at Bill. "I'm so grateful for your time and effort. I know there are people at work who see me as the 'college kid,' and that I got this job because of some executive favor. I'm sure I've made some of my own problems, by being too aggressive, and too intent on doing things my way. I realize that now more than ever . . ."

Randy paused for a moment as he looked out of the window, watching a farmer working in a field alongside the road. Then he continued, "I see now that there's a huge difference between leading and managing. I want and need to be a leader. I want to be the kind of leader that cultivates positive relationships and encourages individuals to go after their dreams. When I started out here, I wanted everyone to know that I knew my stuff. I wanted them to see I'd earned this position, and it wasn't just handed to me. But I'm getting a better idea of what I can do to improve my skills. I'm also beginning to understand that as I lead effectively, not only will I be more effective in my position, but I'll earn the respect and trust of those I work with."

Bill was impressed. He knew Randy had gotten an earful for the last two weeks, and didn't want to detract from the insight he was coming to, so he simply nodded his head in agreement and said, "Sounds like you're figuring it out. It is a process, and you've put forth an incredible effort to learn and be open to new ideas. But you've been willing to put your thoughts and actions on the table and examine them objectively, which is a sign of maturity, confidence, and respect."

Bill finished speaking as they pulled up at his house. Randy let Bill out, and Bill thanked him for driving and reminded him to stop by his office Monday morning. "No problem," Randy said. "I had a great day. See you next week."

As Bill was walking away, he had one last thought to share with Randy. He turned around as Randy started to back up and tapped on the hood. Randy stopped and Bill walked to the passenger side window. Bill leaned in through the window and said, "I just want you to know, you're really doing a good job. I could have kept talking on the way home. I could have told you another story with a lesson behind it. But adding to your thoughts and insights wasn't necessary. Sometimes a leader should just be quiet and let a person have their own moment. This afternoon was your moment, and I learned something from you today."

Mark J. Balzer

Randy had wondered why Bill got out of the truck so quickly; now it made sense. "Thanks Bill; I appreciate it," he said.

Bill replied, "No problem. Enjoy the rest of your weekend. I'll see you Monday morning."

Randy backed out of the driveway and headed home.

Chapter Eleven
(S+A = B) = O

As Bill read his emails, he glanced frequently at his watch. He wondered why Randy wasn't there yet for their meeting. Although they hadn't set an official start time, it was unusual for Randy to be this late. He couldn't help thinking that something was wrong. In the past, Randy had come in first thing in the morning, and it was almost 10:30. Bill knew Randy was at work, because he had seen his truck in the parking lot. He thought he would wait until eleven, and if he hadn't arrived yet, he would go find him.

Bill looked down at his watch again: 10:56. As he began closing out of his email, Randy appeared at the door, out of breath.

"Bill, you're probably wondering where I've been. I apologize for being late, but I had an employee relations issue with Tony Pencek. I just finished up the paperwork and ran up here to see if I could catch you."

Bill smiled and, not wanting Randy to worry about being late, answered, "It's fine, Randy; I've been plenty busy today, and we didn't set a fixed time anyway. Really, you got here at the perfect time. Tell me about Tony."

Taking a moment to catch his breath, Randy sat in the chair, and set down his notebook on the edge of Bill's desk. Then he began to explain the situation. "Tony and Ted Fitzer were picking cases in the pick tunnel on the west side of the building. Apparently, the system directed them to the same location for their order, and they both arrived at the same time. The perfect storm was brewing. Tony told Ted it was his order and he needed to radio the tasker for another order. Ted disagreed and – well, we'll just say words were exchanged.

Kim Rodriquez, our quality supervisor, heard the commotion, and in her words, 'Tony had blown a gasket.' She told Tony to calm down and to go up front immediately. She wanted to diffuse the situation as quickly as possible. Apparently Tony yelled, 'This is bull crap!', picked up a case of baby food and slung it across the aisle, and stormed up front. Obviously, we issued Tony a final written warning. Probably should have fired him, but Bob Torrance talked me out of it. I had a hard time making that concession to Bob, but I figured I should listen to his advice, based on his experience with the company. However, I did tell Tammy Larkins we should start looking for a replacement for Tony. The reality of the situation is that Tony isn't going to make it much longer. I imagine that most people who get that final written warning don't make it here."

Bill picked up his cup of coffee and took a sip, and then just held it with both hands. After a quiet moment, Bill responded, "I think you made the right decision with Tony. How he handled himself was inappropriate and warranted a final written warning, but overall Tony does a good job for us. What makes you believe most people on a final written warning don't make it?"

Randy thought for a moment. In reality, he hadn't been working there for long, and his assumption that "most people on final written warning don't make it" wasn't actually founded on much. So he replied, hesitantly, "In my experience, and I know it is limited, people on a final written warning quit or get fired. Also, considering our corrective action policy, Tony has to go one year without any further rule violation, and with his temper, it'll be a tough road. It's not impossible, but the likelihood of his going one year without another write-up seems very small."

Bill set his cup down and leaned back in his chair. "Randy, think about your conversation with Denise. If you believe he isn't going to make it, won't your perception impact the way you view and treat him? Won't you be determining his value, even his fate, through your actions? Randy, people live up to the faith you have in them."

Randy thought about Bill's last statement. He opened his note book and wrote it down: "People will live up to the faith I have in them." *That sounds good,* he thought, but he still wondered, *What if Tony is so set in his ways that it negates any faith that I have in him?*

"You're probably right," he told Bill, "but my gut instinct is telling me he won't make it. I know that going by a gut reaction probably isn't correct, but I also have to be realistic and prepared for the future. That's all I'm doing. Plus, Tony has to take some ownership in this whole process as well. He can't just put it on my shoulders, can he?"

Bill could see that Randy had a desire to be open to another point of view, but he lacked true experience. So he decided to share a story, to give Randy a different perspective. "My experience is quite different from yours. Several years ago, I hired an employee in our shipping office. She was one of the first people I ever hired here. She quickly became an above-average employee; she was detailed-oriented, with a great sense of urgency and a very pleasant demeanor. It was her second year with us when she got into an argument with a co-worker. It was similar to what happened today between Tony and Ted. It started out as a heated discussion and then evolved into finger-pointing and name-calling, laced with profanity. A supervisor quickly broke up the altercation. We decided their behavior warranted a final written warning. The corrective action policy guidance regarding final written warnings was the same as it is today.

"I sat down with the supervisor and each employee individually, and I'll never forget the discussion I had with the person I hired." Bill could tell Randy was listening intently to the unfolding of events. "We brought her into my office, and I could tell she was remorseful, even somewhat embarrassed by her actions. We issued her the final written warning and she said to me, 'Bill, I'm going to get fired, aren't I?' I wasn't sure what she meant by her question so I asked her, 'Do you mean today?' She said, 'No, not today, but I've seen people get into trouble here and they're gone soon after.'"

Bill paused to take a sip of his coffee; Randy was waiting intently to hear his response to her question. Bill set the cup down and then continued, "I thought about her statement for a moment and told her that she was not going to get fired over this issue. Her behavior was unacceptable, but the purpose of the meeting was to correct the behavior so it wouldn't ever happen again. Once the meeting was over, we would both be moving forward, looking to the future rather than re-living the past. She looked at both of us and asked us if we thought she was a bad employee, and her supervisor told her, 'You were a good employee yesterday, and we know you will be a good employee tomorrow.' She thanked us and apologized for her behavior. You could tell she felt horrible about what had happened and was extremely sorry. Do you remember your first week with us? Didn't you start off your functional training in the shipping office?"

Randy thought for a moment, remembering how helpful Debbie was, that she was so professional and upbeat. "Sure did," he replied happily. "That Debbie Whitehead is the best. She knows her business and she's great to be around. We should start everyone there; she's a great ambassador for our facility. I wish everyone had her work ethic, and even more, her positive attitude."

Bill smiled and leaned back in his chair. "If you check her file, you'll find a final warning in there from about eight years ago."

A big smile came over Randy's face. "No way," he exclaimed. "Debbie Whitehead wasn't the one who did that. She's a class act; she has an even temperament and always acts like a professional. I can't believe under any circumstance that she would act the way you described."

Bill let out a low chuckle and explained, "It was Debbie. It was totally out of character for her, but nonetheless, she lost her temper and her self-control." He picked up his cup of coffee and took a sip; he wanted his statement to sink in with Randy. He wanted Randy to understand that mistakes do not have to define an associate's future. Bill set his cup down and continued, "You're right, Randy, but it also shows you how even very good people can get a little dirty

The People Principles

or wrinkled, just like that twenty-dollar bill Denise talked about on Saturday."

Randy, still shocked that the Debbie he knew was the same Debbie in the story, mused, "It's just so hard to believe she did that; you could knock me over with a feather right now. I guess it means anyone can lose control of their emotions for a minute, can't they?"

"Nobody's perfect, Randy. We all have lapses in judgment and do things we regret. The key is to learn from each experience, and if we're lucky, we have a leader that understands this and won't hold it against us. Now, let me ask you, do you think your attitude toward Tony is fair to him?"

Randy knew the answer immediately, and he knew that Bill knew it as well. He also knew this could be a defining moment in the shaping of his leadership style. Randy humbly shook his head no, and said, "What I need to do is put the Tony issue behind me and treat him like I did before the write-up."

Bill nodded his head in agreement. "The sole purpose of corrective action is to help people get back to an acceptable job performance, not to punish them. Punishment just creates the three A's."

"The three A's . . . What are the three A's, Bill?"

"The three A's are absence, apathy, and anger. There isn't an upside to any of them. You need to remember, we hire people here to make them successful. We don't hire people to fire people. People are going to use poor judgment from time to time. Our role is to correct the behavior and move on; everyone deserves a second chance. Good leaders have a short memory. Poor leaders put people in the doghouse and never let them out. That just isn't fair, is it?"

Randy didn't hesitate; he knew he didn't want to fall into the trap of holding grudges. He looked at Bill and said, "I agree that Tony deserves a second chance. I discussed his behavior with him. He knows it was inappropriate, and I need to move forward. I need to give him a chance to redeem himself and help him be successful here. You're right that holding this against him and having the perception that he isn't going to make it will impact the way I treat him. Isn't that the Pygmalion effect we discussed the other day?"

"Very good, Randy, it sure is. You'll create a self-fulfilling prophecy for Tony, and he'll act accordingly." Bill thought of one more point he wanted to share, to help drive his point home. "Randy, you know how our organization is strong in the area of cross-training?"

Randy nodded. "Oh yeah, I'm well aware."

Bill continued, "Well, there might be a time when you end up with an associate that has 'a reputation,' and their supervisor will warn you to watch out for that person."

Randy knew exactly what Bill was talking about; he remembered just such a situation coming up only the week before. "Yes, I've seen that happen."

Bill said, "Well, I met a supervisor in Indianapolis that has a positive way of handling this kind of situation. He makes it a practice to meet with the so-called problem associate, and he tells them one simple fact. He tells them that when they come to his area, they start with a clean slate. He tells them that whatever happened in the other department stays in that department, unless they bring it with them. He tells them that he can't change their past, and he can't get rid of it. But, together, they can do something positive about their future. Randy, that supervisor understands the power and potential of moving forward."

Randy could see how that could be a positive, defining moment for both parties. "I'll follow that example, Bill. It really makes good sense to give someone a fresh start."

Randy could see how things were coming together, but this brought up another question he had about the Tony situation. He asked, "Can we discuss the process of dealing with situations like this one? Bob was a big help in talking with Tony. I'm not sure the conversation would have gone as well if it were just me. I simply don't have a good understanding of the whole process."

Bill could see Randy's mind turning, and was more than happy to elaborate about such a useful leadership tool. "Sure thing, Randy; let me show you." He grabbed a marker and wrote on the whiteboard:

$$(S + A = B) = 0.$$

Randy grabbed his notebook and joked, "Are you going to give me a math lesson or a feedback lesson?"

Bill laughed. "Very funny. Actually, this is a formula I came up with a few years back to frame up the process of giving feedback. The S is for situational and self-awareness. The first thing you need to think about is the situation. What occurred, and what needs to be done? Second, you need to be aware of your emotions and feelings, and the emotions and feelings of the other person or people involved. Your emotions and feelings are going to dictate the A. The A is for attitude. If you let your emotions dictate the situation, it usually affects your attitude. Giving feedback isn't your opportunity to take out bring out your arsenal and crush people. John Maxwell's book *Winning with People* has a law that states, 'Never use a hammer to swat a fly off someone's head.'"

Randy laughed out loud. "Bill, you always do have some good anecdote to make your point."

"I'm not sure about that." Bill walked over to the coffee pot and filled his cup while Randy wrote down the formula, and the quotation. Then he continued. "Next, you need to take into account the other person's feelings. If you tell the person you need to see them in your office right away, what do you think they're feeling and thinking?"

Randy remembered his old manager and said, "I know I'd be thinking, what did I do wrong? I'd probably be nervous about meeting you."

"So, Randy, you wouldn't be thinking that your boss has finally recognized your talents and abilities and you're getting promoted today?" Bill asked with a smile.

"I don't think so. The last thing I'd be thinking about is a promotion. I'd be stressed out," responded Randy.

"Okay, now, if you were the employee and your boss told you to come up to her office right away, and you knew you had made a mistake, how would you like to be treated?"

"I'd like her to treat me with respect. I'd like my manager to explain what I did wrong and how to correct it. I'd hope she would help me see how I can avoid doing it again."

Bill asked Randy to write his next statement down. "When giving feedback, you don't want to come across as a dispenser of punishment; you do want to come across as a coach." Bill waited for Randy to finish writing. Then he continued, "I don't believe that people wake up in the morning and say, 'I can't wait to get to work today and make some mistakes.' But the best opportunity to coach a person is immediately after they've done something wrong. This is when people are most receptive to instruction. We have to remember, people aren't perfect, and we all make mistakes."

"That makes sense to me. I want to learn from my mistakes, and I'd be open to my supervisor's guidance."

"Good; we're on the same page. Now this next point is critical in the feedback process. The one word you need to avoid when starting the conversation is the word 'you.' Why do you think that might be?"

Randy responded, his tone hesitant, "It seems like it would immediately put the person in a defensive mode . . . ?"

"Are you asking me Randy, or is that your answer?"

Randy thought for a second and then said with a crafty grin, "That's my final answer."

Bill chuckled and nodded in confirmation. "Correct! It puts the person on the defensive. The next word you should avoid using is the word 'but.' The word 'but' is an eraser word."

Randy looked puzzled. "An eraser word? What does that mean? I learned in a training class that communication is irreversible. Once you say something, you can't take it back; is there a way to erase your words? I'm lost."

"Your instructor was correct that communication is irreversible, but stay with me on this one, and you'll see what I mean by an eraser word. When you use the word 'but,' everything you say before the word 'but' is erased, and people will mostly remember what you say after the word 'but'." Randy tried to interrupt, but Bill continued with his explanation. "For example: 'Randy you're doing a great job, but you need to be more detail-oriented. Some of your work is sloppy.' What will you remember? The first part of the sentence before the word 'but', or the second part of the sentence?"

Randy was starting to get it. "Definitely the second part. Heck, I forgot what you just said before the 'but.' All I remember is my work is sloppy."

Bill nodded slightly and continued. "Most people do. I said it, and I can't reverse it, but you didn't remember the first part of the sentence; you only remembered the second part. Communication is irreversible, but it's what the other person hears and remembers that's important. Are you still with me?"

"I am still with you. Still, though, your intent was to give some praise first, so your intent was good, wasn't it?"

Bill knew what Randy was asking, yet he also knew how many times people in leadership roles missed this important point. He began, "You may want to write this down." Randy got his pen ready. "The effectiveness of communication is not evaluated by the speaker's intent; it is measured by what the other person hears. I can't tell you how many people explain they were misunderstood because it was not their intent to hurt someone else's feelings. But does their intent really matter to the person they hurt?"

"No, it doesn't; we need to make sure we have the right approach and choose our words carefully."

"Exactly, Randy. Words do matter, and how they are delivered determines their effectiveness. Let's continue with the formula. Now, having awareness of yourself and others will help you have the right attitude for providing feedback. Your mindset should be to correct behavior, not to belittle the person."

Randy interrupted by politely lifting his left hand. "Bill, would you please repeat your last statement?"

Bill said eagerly, "Sure I will. Your mindset should be to correct behavior not to belittle the person." He gave Randy a moment to write, then continued, "Whatever your attitude is going into the interaction will dictate B. B stands for behavior. If my attitude is right, my behavior will be right. I won't come across as the disciplinarian; I'll come across as a coach. If my attitude is to inflict pain, then my behavior will inflict pain. The O stands for outcome. If I am aware of the situation, have the right attitude for giving feedback, and behave like a coach, then the outcome should be positive. I remember the process by using the formula $(S + A = B) = O$. Does the formula make sense to you now?"

Randy replied, "It does. Can I have just a moment to think through all this?"

Bill replied, "Take your time, and then we'll wrap this up; I have a meeting with Steve".

Randy nodded, looking at the board and then his notes. He was amazed at the simplicity of the process, and yet he could understand how easy it might for people in leadership roles to miss the main point, that they should work "to correct behavior, not to belittle the person." By consistently applying these principles with the right attitude and having the receivers' best interest at heart, it would possible to have effective and meaningful communication even in difficult situations.

Randy spoke up. "I think I'm getting it, and I can see the benefits of communicating with these principles as my foundation.

Bill replied, "That's exactly right." He turned back to the white board and wrote out the complete formula.

$$S + A = B + O$$

S – Situation and self-awareness
A – Attitude
B – Behavior
O – Outcome

Then he looked at Randy and asked, "Does this help to make it clearer?"

Randy finished writing and replied, "Yes, and it's easier to remember." He had one last question, since he knew Bill had to get to his meeting. "Okay, now that you've got all those things in order, do you have some kind of material that I could go over to learn how to conduct a feedback session?"

Bill smiled and took a book out of his desk. "This will be very helpful; just what you're looking for. Read the fourth chapter, 'Crucial Interactions.' It outlines constructive feedback. If you jot down any questions you have, we can discuss it later."

Bill looked at his watch and found it was almost noon. He stood up and said, "I need to run to my lunch meeting with Steve; you know how he is about punctuality."

Mark J. Balzer

Randy laughed. "I sure do. Thanks again, Bill." He closed his notebook and they walked out of Bill's office together.

Conclusion
Pay it forward

Six months had passed since Bill and Randy began working together, and Randy had progressed very well in his development. He was perceived by both the leadership team and employees as an excellent supervisor, and his team was well on its way to completing the first phase of their three-year vision. Bill had moved on to a regional role for the Northeastern part of the United Sates, supporting fifteen other sites, but he still kept his office at the Dunkirk facility. His new role had him on the road a lot and he usually spent only two or three days a month at Dunkirk Distribution. It was unusual for him to be in Dunkirk on a Monday, but on this particular Monday, Steve had requested a meeting to discuss succession planning with him.

As Bill parked his car, he heard someone yelling from across the parking lot, "Bill! Bill, over here!" It was Randy Sysol, waving his hand as he approached him. "I haven't seen you in a month!" he said with a smile. "I knew you were going to be here today."

Bill was puzzled because the only person he kept up-to-date on his schedule was Steve. "Good to see you, Randy. How did you know I was coming in today?"

"You've got a meeting with Steve this morning, and I'll be joining you. By the way, how's the new job going?"

"I love it. It's challenging, and I've met so many wonderful people throughout the region. We have good people working for our company; it's amazing, the quality of people we've been able to attract to the organization. It makes me proud to be an employee of Globalistics. The travel is a little rough at times, and it's been a big change for Casey and me, but we're adjusting. I love going out to Boston. My son is enrolled at Boston College, so I get a chance to spend some time with him. Overall though, I don't have any complaints. You know my philosophy on life. When I wake up in the morning, it's the start of a good day, and when I know my family is alive and well, the day just gets better. And when my pass key lets me into a facility, my life is good. I'm alive, my family's alive, and I have a job. What else do I need? Everything after that is gravy. Enough about me, though; how's your world?"

"Oh, I'm living the dream. If I was doing any better, I'd be you, Bill!"

Both Bill and Randy laughed and Bill said, "Wow, that good? I'm impressed."

"In all seriousness, things have really come together for me. The team is doing great. We've made huge strides with implementing our vision, though the team should get most of the credit for that. Brian Fellinger is now a cycle counter, and he's doing great, so his development plan worked, and Tony Pencek is still with us. He really came around after the write-up. He actually thanked me for treating him with respect. He thought I'd be gunning for him after the incident, and he appreciated the fact I didn't hold it against him. He's one of my biggest supporters now; I can't believe I was ready to write him off. It's great. I know I've said this a few times, but without your mentoring, I'm not sure I would have made it. Thanks again, Bill."

"Randy, all I did was to provide you with the tools; you were open to the coaching, you worked hard making the necessary changes to your leadership style, and you got the results you wanted. I've shared my insights with people throughout my career, but whether the coaching is successful or not depends on the individual. Most people know what they need to improve, but many people lack the discipline necessary to make the changes. People may want to change, but they don't always have the 'want power' and commitment to do it. They have to understand that eighty percent of an individual's development rests squarely on their shoulders, and the unfortunate fact is that people won't, and I emphasize the word *won't*, do what it takes to grow and develop. It's not that they can't, they just won't.

Too many people expect the company or their manager to take responsibility for their development. It doesn't work that way. Great opportunities aren't lost; they're given to someone else. I am really proud of you. I've heard many positive comments about you over the last few months; you should be proud of your accomplishments."

"Thanks for the feedback, Bill. Like you always said, leadership is a journey, not a destination. I'm off to a good start on my journey, but I still have a long way to go. By the way, I took your advice when we were wrapping up the feedback discussion in your office, and I'm reading a few leadership books every month and keeping a journal of what I learn. I'm trying to apply concepts from the books in my leadership ability."

"I'm glad you're reading. It's an inexpensive, self-paced way to develop yourself. The more I read and learn about leadership, the more I realize I have so much more to learn. It's a challenge every day, but I owe it to the people that work for me to develop myself to the fullest. Since I determine the quality of their work life, they deserve the best possible leader I can be. I made a commitment a long time ago to give a one-hundred percent effort to my people, one-hundred percent of my time. It doesn't mean I don't make mistakes, but they deserve my best. After all, my performance is directly linked to their performance."

Bill paused for a split second and realized he was getting on his soapbox. He grinned sheepishly and raised a hand. "Sorry, you probably don't want another lecture from me on leadership, but it is such a passion of mine."

Randy reassured him, "Bill, to be honest, I would have been disappointed if you didn't share some of your thoughts with me. I miss our coaching sessions. I wish you could spend more time at Dunkirk."

Bill nodded, thinking that he missed their time together as well. "I appreciate that. There are times on the road when I really miss this place. Oh yeah, before I forget, if you haven't signed up for our

E-learning system yet, do it. It's a great web-based development tool that gives you accessibility 24/7. There are over five hundred courses available. Our people really need to take advantage of it."

Randy chuckled and told him, "I signed up two weeks ago, and I've already completed a class on creating development plans. It was great."

Bill was pleasantly surprised, and yet not really surprised at all. He said, "Randy that was a smart move on your part, and it's good to see that you took the initiative." He checked his watch and added, "Well, we better get moving, or we'll be late for the meeting." As they began walking, he asked, "Not to be nosey or disrespectful, but why are you coming to this meeting on succession planning?"

"You'll have to wait until we talk to Steve, but I think you'll be both surprised and happy."

Bill and Randy made their way up the stairs to the second floor, to the Marauder Conference Room next to Steve's office. They found Steve already there, the succession planning documents on the table in a neat pile.

Steve walked over and shook their hands. "Glad you both could make it today." He looked at Bill and added, "Bill, you're probably wondering why I invited Randy to join us today."

"I am, though I'm glad you did. We had a chance to talk for a minute in the parking lot, and it gave us a chance to get caught up. With my schedule, I won't be back here for six weeks. You heard about the labor issues in Frederick, didn't you?"

Steve motioned for everyone to have a seat. "I did, so I know you'll have your hands full. That's the primary reason I invited Randy today. I wanted to make sure you had a chance to see him. You guys ready to start?" Both men said yes. "Let's start with Randy, and after that we can get into the succession planning document. First of all, I'd like to thank both of you for your effort over the last half-year. Bill, your development plan for Randy was very helpful, and Randy, your willingness and commitment to implement it back at work has paid off for you. I still remember when you handed me the plan that consisted of *The Wizard of Oz*, fishing lures, green beans, and the rest. I thought you'd lost it."

"I remember that meeting," Bill said. "The look on your face was priceless, but to your credit, you trusted my judgment and let me work my plan."

Steve leaned back in his chair and gave a soft laugh. "I wish I could say that's just what great leaders do, but let's be honest; I didn't have any other choice, did I?"

Bill responded with a smile . "I see your point, but nevertheless, you gave me the freedom I needed to work the plan."

Steve agreed with a nod and continued, "Thanks, Bill. Now let's discuss why Mr. Sysol has joined us today. Bill, as you know, we were recently awarded the contract for the Moreland Plastics Network. The network will consist of seven warehouses throughout the United States and an in-plant operation managing their vendor supplies. The location for their Midwest facility is in Indianapolis, and it will employ eight hundred people. The Moreland executive team felt the need for a small overflow supply site in the Midwest, which they're planning to base in Davenport, Iowa. It will be a two-shift operation with roughly forty people. The facility needs a second-shift operation manager with a strong background in inventory control."

Steve paused for a moment and then looked at Randy, continuing, "Based on Randy's performance here, I recommended him for the position. He interviewed, and you're looking at the new operations manager for the Davenport Supply Center."

Bill's eyes opened huge and he smiled from ear to ear. "Congratulations, Mr. Sysol! What a great opportunity for you – and you'll be closer to home. Now that's a win-win situation! All your hard work has paid off for you. This makes my day. You should be proud of yourself!"

Randy smiled and said confidently, "I'm proud of what I've accomplished here, but I realize that without your coaching and the incredible effort of a wonderful team, this wouldn't be possible. I really am going to miss everyone here, and I hope we do stay in touch."

"Randy, you can call me anytime you need help, or just want to talk. Don't ever hesitate. So, when will you be leaving the site?"

"Judy Kaiser, the general manager, needs me there in three weeks. I wanted you to know before I told and thanked my team. I didn't want you to hear about it from anyone else, and with your workload, this was probably my only chance to tell you."

Bill was very proud of Randy. He was happy to see how things had turned around for him. He also was impressed with the maturity and commitment Randy had show over the last six months. "I'm so glad you did. I'll be out of town that week, but I'll be back on the weekend, and I'd love to throw you a going-away party at my house. We can have a barbeque in my backyard, and the tomatoes and beans are ready to be picked, so you can enjoy some of the fruits of your labor. We'll invite Steve, Denise, and Nick for sure, and anyone else you would like to have there."

Randy was truly grateful for Bill's warm gesture, and humbled as well; he knew how busy Bill was, and it meant a lot. "You don't have to do that for me, Bill," he told him. "I don't want to cut into your time with your family. You've given me enough already."

Bill could see that Randy didn't want to put him out, but this was a big deal, and a testament to Randy's hard work. "I know I don't have to; I want to. So it's set, Saturday night at five o'clock at my house. I'll set up the volleyball net and the cornhole boards, and some horseshoes. It'll be a blast. Just let me know who else should be invited."

Randy could see that Bill's mind was made up, and it really was something he wanted to do. "I really do appreciate this, Bill. I've been wondering about the garden; are you going to win the competition with your neighbor?"

"It's going to be close," replied Bill.

Steve looked at both men. "Sounds like a plan. Randy, do you need anything else from Bill before we let you get back to work?"

Randy knew it would be a while before he would see Bill again and wanted to give him a chance to share any last thoughts. "Any final advice for me?"

Bill thought for a moment. "Randy, continue growing every day. Anytime training is offered, take it. Continue reading books, read trade journals, use E-learning, and network with other leaders in the organization. Learning is a life-long process; be a life-long learner. I do have one favor to ask of you."

Randy was quick to reply, "Whatever you need, I'll do it."

"When I was your age, someone took me under his wing and gave me the guidance I needed at a crucial point in my career. If it weren't for him, I'm not sure I'd be in the position I am today. Because of his selfless and dedicated commitment, I made a commitment to myself: I would pay him back by helping others grow in their career. As you grow and gain more experience, someone is going to need your help, and you can show your appreciation by paying it forward."

Randy asked, a little confused, "Pay it forward?"

"Yes," Bill replied, "Pay the system back. Take what you've learned, and what you'll continue to learn in your career, and pay it forward to the next generation of leaders. Hopefully they'll pay it forward as well. It keeps the development cycle of our culture intact."

Randy knew exactly what Bill was saying; he was, after all, a beneficiary of the commitment Bill had made. "Bill, you have my commitment to pay it forward."

Steve slid his chair back a bit to stand up; Bill and Randy followed his lead. Randy walked around the table and shook hands with Bill and Steve, thanking them again for their time. Then he turned towards the door and left the office.

Steve smiled, looking at Bill, and said, "The kid's going to make it. You know something, I hear about leadership in one way or another pretty much every week. I've been to the classes just like everyone else. I gotta be honest, the majority of the time, it just seems like a hollow cliché. But as I've watched you work with Randy, I've seen the true-to-life results of solid leadership principles in practice. Hard to believe this whole adventure started with Sean Murphy being so adamant about Randy's success in the company. Even though Randy was doing so poorly as a supervisor, Murphy's determination that failure was not an option, that Randy was a 'can't miss' candidate, really had me worried. To be completely honest, his expectations for Randy really had me at a loss."

Bill, leaning against the table, smiled and replied, "Steve, it really was a group effort. I was blessed to have real-life events to relate to that gave merit to each of the principles I wanted to teach him. It really makes a difference when I can say to someone: 'These principles work, and here is a real-life situation to prove it.'"

Steve nodded in agreement and continued, "That's very true, and as a leader, I had to trust in you and your ability to make things right. I must also admit that trusting you was possible because of your own example of leadership, which I've seen over the years. It really does come down to effectively leading people in a direction that ensures them the opportunity for success. Granted, I also realize that it will be up to them to consistently apply the principles that have been presented to them."

Steve paused for a moment, and let out a soft sigh. Then he continued, "I apologize for not giving you the real support you deserved. It was easier to question and doubt you, than to trust in your ability and desire to develop an associate. I assure you, though, I've learned something from this experience as well. We have plenty of Randys in this facility, though their names may be Stephanie, Linda, or Juan, and every one of them has potential. It shouldn't take the president of the company giving me an order to develop an associate. It should be one of the driving forces within any leadership team, and with your help, I'd like to bring this message home, starting with our facility."

Bill was moved by Steve's candor and humility. He knew this was a learning opportunity for everyone involved, and was happy to make sure that everyone had the opportunity to be the most they could be. He leaned over the table and reached out to shake hands with Steve, saying, "Steve, you have a deal. I'd love to see everyone in our organization have the opportunity to grow and develop into the person they were meant to be."

Steve laughed and said, "Great. I'm looking forward to the journey. Now, let's get started reviewing this document."

Afterward

Leadership is not a place to be; it is a journey. We owe it to the people we lead every day to be the best leader possible. Be a life-long learner. Too many people buy into the notion of thinking they know it all. These people eventually become dinosaurs, and their skills become obsolete. Just like the dinosaurs, they go extinct.

As with any journey, the first step is the most important. Without the first step, no journey can begin, nor be fulfilled. Most people don't fail in their leadership journey; they quit before they ever get started. Whether you are a brand-new leader like Randy Sysol or an experienced leader like Bill Crocoll, take responsibility for your own development. You're responsible for your career, and your development falls on your shoulders. Have the discipline and commitment to take the first step.

Many leaders don't know how or where to start. "Where do I begin the leadership journey?" is a common question often asked to people in the learning and development field. Use the MapQuest analogy from the book. Where am I, and where do I need to go? Commit your answers to writing, and keep them visible so you can review them daily. Mentally covering the plan won't work; you need your plan in a concrete form. Develop an action plan to apply the skills.

Keep your focus, have discipline, and make a commitment to your journey. Remember, your destiny is in your hands. Make this year an extraordinary year.

I wish you the best of luck in your journey, and I hope you enjoyed this book as much as I enjoyed writing it and sharing it with you.

Acknowledgements

First, thanks to my Lord and Savior Jesus Christ for blessing me with the ability to write this book.

Thanks to my lovely wife Tammy; without her love, support, and guidance throughout my life and career, my world would not be possible. She is my strength. To my three children, Ralston, Markus, and Kensey, thank you for your love and support in my life. It's kept me focused on my priorities. You make me proud to be your father.

Thanks to my mother and father, Jeanette and Andy Balzer, who instilled me with great values and were great role models for me to follow. Also, a special thanks to Aunt Elsie and Uncle Lee Damon, my second parents.

Thanks to Robert and Mary Larkins, my in-laws, who have provided me with guidance throughout my married life.

Thanks to by brothers Andy, Mike, and Rick and to my cousins Leigh Ellen and Tom for all the love them gave me throughout my life.

Special thanks to Mary France, Jim Arbogast, Fran Ketter, Ashley Huffman, and Daniel Ely, who provided me with encouragement to continue writing *The People Principles*, and their many hours spent proofing the book. I am so lucky and blessed to be surrounded daily by such wonderful people.

Thanks to Chris Sims who transformed me from a HR person to a business person working in HR.

Thanks to Rob Rosenberg who talked me into taking the Learning and Development role at Exel and all your support throughout the years.

Thanks to the senior leadership team at Exel for allowing me train and develop the amazing people at our company. Your support for my team is incredible!

Last but not least, thanks all my wonderful friends, colleagues, and all the people I've had the opportunity to work with and train over the years.